65 Goalkeeper Training Exercises

Modern Games-Based Soccer Drills for Shot Stopping, Footwork, Distribution, and More

Andy Elleray

Oakamoor
Publishing

Published by Oakamoor Publishing, an imprint of Bennion Kearny Limited
6 Woodside
Churnet View Road
Oakamoor
Staffordshire
ST10 3AE

www.BennionKearny.com

About This Book

This book utilises curated content from Andy Elleray's acclaimed book *Scientific Approaches to Goalkeeping in Football: A practical perspective on the most unique position in sport.*

If you would like to upgrade to the *Scientific Approaches* book, a discounted version is available direct from the publisher.

Please email **Info@BennionKearny.com** for details.

About the Author

Andy Elleray is a goalkeeping coach who also specializes in performance analysis and sports science. His former clubs include Cheltenham Town, Liverpool and Chelsea, working at different levels, and in a variety of roles. He is currently responsible for the goalkeeping development at Birmingham City Ladies Football Club where he works at all levels of the club with youth international goalkeepers in the female game. He is also involved in different regional and youth international coaching environments. Holding UEFA qualifications, Youth Awards, and a Master's degree, Andy blends different approaches into his current coaching projects.

Previously he has undertaken research projects and presented at International sports and football conferences over Europe on various elements of goalkeeping in Football. These include 'the ISPAS (Performance Analysis Congress), Intentional Goalkeeping Conference, and the Science & Football Conference. His work has taken him into Sports Science Lectureship over the past two years.

Table of Contents

Games-Based Goalkeeper Training..1
An Introduction to Teaching Games for Understanding 3
The Games 5
Goalkeeping Bulldog 6
American Goalkeeper.. 8
Coloured Cone Games.. 10
Dodgy Keeper! 11
Circuit Training.. 13
Goalkeeper's Volleyball... 15
Goalkeeper's Tennis 17
Goalkeeper's Tennis (No Hands)... 19
Keeper Combat 21
Basket-Keeper.. 23
Bench-ball.. 24
Face and Dive 26
Follow the Keeper 28
Lines 29
Piggy in the Middle 30
Back Ball/Knees.. 32
Keeper's Union.. 33
Mini Match 36
Warm Up Goals 38
Touch Rugby.. 39
Keeping with the Hands 41
Games-Based Handling and Shot Stopping 43
Four Goal Game... 43
Triangle Goal Game 45
Double Team.. 47
Quick Attack 49
The Circle of Saves 51
Team Keeper.. 52
Own Goal.. 54
Zones 56
Outnumbered 58
Multi-Goal.. 60
Get To The Next One! 62
Backwards and Forwards.. 64
Goalie-Ball.. 65
The Pit... 67
Choices.. 69
Back to Back 70
Inside Out... 72

Testing the Angles..73

Boomerang..74

Back 2 Goal..77

Stay in Control!..78

Beat the Goalie..80

Ball Out!...81

Games-Based Footwork and Distribution **83**

Obstacle Course...83

Slalom..85

Moving Goal...86

The 'Footlympics'...87

Footlympics: Jumping Circuit 87

Footlympics: Get The Ball...89

Footlympics: Coloured Feet 90

Footlympics: Andy Agility Meter..93

Footlympics: Coloured Batak...95

Back Pass...97

No Bounce 99

Goalkeeper Bowls 101

Distribution Gates..102

Accuracy...103

1v1 Situations **106**

Gate Keeper...106

Keeper in the Middle...108

Crocodiles..109

Parallel Goals 111

Reaction 1 v 1 112

Goals Galore..113

Crossing 115

Cross Goal...115

Don't Cross Me! 117

Summary **118**

Bonus Section..**119**

Other Coaching Books..**127**

Games-Based Goalkeeper Training

In my career I've had the privilege of working with a host of different ages and abilities, not just within goalkeeping and football but also across numerous other sports. I would say - like most coaches - that my experiences have helped shape the way I approach my coaching and the philosophy which I endeavour to follow.

Having taken numerous coaching courses in football, handball, and basketball to name but a few, the content of these courses have given me a platform to build my approach utilising different drills, skills, and techniques from each.

From the outset I will stress that standard technical drills *still have an important role to play in goalkeeper development*. What this coaching concept aims to do is offer an alternative to the drill-based sessions - *not replace them*. Training must replicate match situations for a number of reasons but most importantly for decision making – the concept takes specific skills for goalkeeping into different environments whilst still building up skill acquisition and familiarity. A key aim of the training theory is to produce skilful goalkeepers, not just technical goalkeepers. By this I mean that we should be training keepers not to simply be proficient in handling, footwork and positioning in isolated situations, they need to adaptable, reactive, and able to utilise different goalkeeping skills within different match-specific scenarios.

It is important, from a physical viewpoint, that games are played in a short, sharp and intense manner. Some of the games can be quite chaotic, so make sure there are good rest periods just as players would face in a match – periods of inactivity with good amounts of physical recovery time.

This games-based approach can perhaps be likened to the goalkeeping version of Futsal, where the player receives more touches and time on the ball. Futsal is a fantastic game for goalkeepers for working on close control, being pressured on the ball, playing as a sweeper, and shifting the ball with sharpness - not to mention enhancing reactions through quickfire shooting and saving the ball (not just with hands). Some games involve the goalkeeper without the ball, which is extremely common in matches. Necessary concentration must be applied in these environments!

The games-based methodology has been used successfully in many different environments. From grassroots novice goalkeeping centres right up to elite youth level – each level of coach will be able to take certain games from the ones shown with beginner coaches (in my experience) using the games to develop basic goalkeeping skills.

So, let's crack on and get this ball rolling...

An Introduction to Teaching Games for Understanding

One method of teaching I was exposed to early on in my University life was that of TGfU (Teaching Games for Understanding). Brought to light by Bunker and Thorpe in the early 1980s and perfected by people such as John Allpress (The FA) and Lynn Kidman, this philosophy is focused around the game (or sport) being the teacher with the participant taking a direct involvement in learning. The way this works is that the coach sets up the environment and lets participants make decisions for themselves rather than orchestrating proceedings directly. The coach does so by asking specific questions and setting up game-specific scenarios which often seem chaotic but which aim to replicate a match situation. These questions might include: "How can you be in a more effective position to save that ball?", "By changing your position can you help the team?", "What technique might be more appropriate to save the ball?", or "What commands does your teammate need in this situation?"

For some of the games, lists of potential coaching points that may arise have been included. Although not every single coaching point has been written down, the ones included should give you a good basis to start the games, providing cues as to what situations might arise and staying aware of the goalkeeping demands within the games. Along with these, a few suggested starting points are included (for some of the games) that are designed to put the coach in a position to organise matters effectively.

This way of learning is different to most current goalkeeper training which involves technical practices isolated in the goal or penalty areas. These TGfU games (if *purposeful*) offer an alternative approach that complements current goalkeeping work. Specific drill work which focuses on a topic or movement is still useful when the situation requires it, but it is important to remember that athletes learn better when the environment is realistic.

Much of games-based goalkeeper training is designed for coaches who have a large group of goalkeepers to work with. With large numbers, it is very hard to do small technical practices in goals, because of space constraints and having so many goalkeepers not working (or only working as servers or passive players).

Games-based goalkeeper training combines physical, psychological, technical, tactical and social skills in small situations that a goalkeeper will face in games. These include 1v1s, communicating with the defence, decision making, shot stopping, and more.

Goalkeeping is not just about going in goal and someone kicking a ball at you. There is so much more to the position in the modern game: a goalkeeper must be able to use their feet, communicate effectively with the team as a whole, have an in-depth understanding of football, and prove able to read the game situation. Goalkeepers will be working on areas of their game relevant to their position without even knowing it because they will be made to think quickly and do what comes naturally to them. They will be learning to cope with new and challenging situations in these games and how to work as a team to win points or solve a problem.

It should be noted that most of these games are inclusive for all keepers in the training environment as most of them only require balls, cones, bibs and a coach with a creative and imaginative mind. The other equipment is easily replicated if certain pieces cannot be found; cone substitutes are a more than useful replacement for many situations.

The Games

For each game listed, the purposes are referenced in the accompanying explanations so coaches can tailor their sessions accordingly. The set distances, diameters, and lengths are not usually stated because it will be up to the coach to decide this through identifying their goalkeepers' needs.

If working on short reaction saves then decrease the length of the working zone, and do the opposite for long range work. If there are a large number of players, then make areas bigger and add in more goals. All the games are flexible and adaptable depending on the age, ability, and number of goalkeepers in the group.

Knowing your goalkeepers' needs is very important, so if you wish to challenge them - make goals bigger, areas tighter, and apply stricter rules such as deducted points/goals or lives for basic errors. This is especially applicable for advanced players, but it is up to the coach, or at times the goalkeeper's themselves, to choose the appropriate scenarios.

To make the games easier, simply make the goals smaller, increase target areas or make exceptions for good play to build up a goalkeeper's confidence.

At the end of the day, goalkeeper enjoyment, development, and progression are all extremely important and through the games in this book you will find that all goalkeeper areas will be worked upon in a fun and safe environment. And in a good learning atmosphere!

The games will be broken down by name, explanation, the areas of goalkeeping worked on, and finally the setup. Let's begin!

Goalkeeping Bulldog

Explanation

The aim of this exercise is for the runners to evade the bulldogs and to get to a designated area of safety or a target. The bulldogs have to tag the runners, or remove a bib tucked into the runners' shorts or trousers. This is a non-contact exercise.

Goalkeeping Bulldog benefits goalkeepers because it gets them moving and warmed up both mentally and physically for the session ahead.

When running this game - overloading either side can make life more challenging for the bulldogs. Giving the runners a ball to get across to the other side will also test the participants' teamwork and communication skills.

Within the game certain tactics can be used; for example assembling a wall to block the runners which can relate directly to a match situation with free kicks. Goalkeeping Bulldog is also excellent in 'new sessions' where it can be used as an icebreaker to get to know everyone in the group.

Areas Worked

- General agility
- Speed/quick footwork
- Decision making
- Communication
- Teamwork – when teamwork is mentioned, within games, it implies that goalkeepers are working towards a common goal. The coach could ask questions such as "How can your positioning here benefit your team?" or "If you were to pass there, how can your team build up an attack?"

Typical Setup

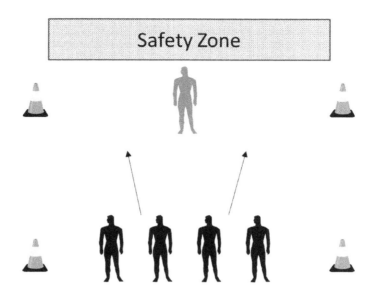

Alternative Setup

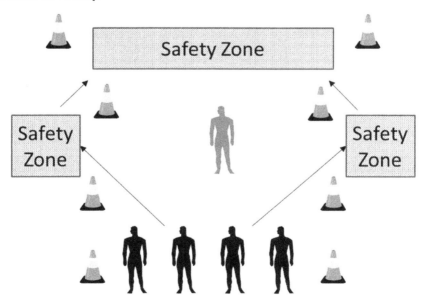

American Goalkeeper

Explanation

The aim with American Goalkeeper is for the team in possession of the ball to reach the opposition's end zone (or to reach an area on, or beyond, the end of the grid). It's a non-contact game. As in a match situation, only 6 seconds are allowed with the ball in hand whilst no running is allowed with the ball - only a pivot step in all directions.

There are many variations of this game, for instance, you can use:

- Different sizes or types of ball
- Only allow certain types of throw to be used
- Have someone permanently in an end zone (organising the team)
- Play with end zones scattered around the pitch
- No overhead height
- Use feet instead of hands (no pivot involved)
- If the ball is dropped then turnover ball (working on handling)
- Put a dividing line half way across the pitch – this will make one goalkeeper stay back orchestrating the team

Areas Worked

- Basic handling
- Communication
- Ball distribution
- Reactive agility
- General motor skills
- Communication (specific to goalkeeping)

Potential Coaching Points

- Hand shapes on catching the balls
- Weight, accuracy, and appropriateness of passes
- Diving technique
- Tone and directness of communication
- The challenge of high balls (body position and approach)

Game Starting Positions

- Coach starts with the ball and plays to one of the teams (varying heights)
- Team who is scored against restarts the play
- If the ball goes out on the sideline, the team who didn't touch it last restarts

Typical Setup

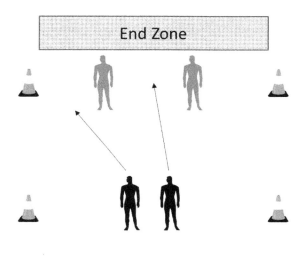

Alternative Setup

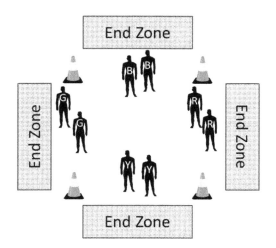

Coloured Cone Games

Explanation

Each goalkeeper moves around the grid changing direction and taking small short steps like a goalkeeper would move. When a coloured cone is called, they will go and touch that cone as quickly as possible then return to moving around inside the grid.

There will be balls placed around the outside so when "ball" is shouted the keepers will dive on the nearest ball. Different instructions must be adhered to in the grid, such as "jump" or "get low". Two grids may be used to avoid clutter in one.

This is very effective as a warm up because keepers need to engage their brains alongside physical movement and get their bodies ready for the session ahead.

Additional hurdles and exercises can be placed in and around the grid and specific goalkeeper movements called.

Areas Worked

- Reaction time
- Decision making
- Quick feet
- Power movements

Typical Setup

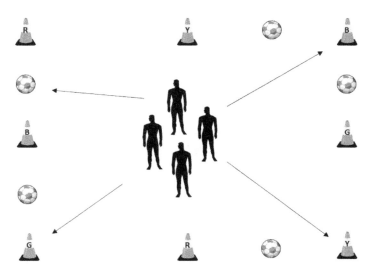

Dodgy Keeper!

Explanation

Like the traditional Dodgeball game, the goalkeeper has to dodge the ball and make it across a designated area.

Areas Worked

- Reactions: With balls flying everywhere the keeper needs to be able to react to catch a ball, move sharply to avoid it, or use the ball in his hands to deflect it away.
- Decision Making: The keeper needs to decide when to throw the ball and how to do it, when to avoid the ball or catch it, and how to organise the team (defence).
- Footwork: To get in line with the ball when catching, to avoid the ball, move towards the opponent when aiming. It is also valuable for getting around the pitch quickly, effectively, and with purpose.
- Handling: The basic catching of a ball doesn't change in any sport - you need to have a basic stance and catching shape to hold the ball.
- Communication: To organise a team as the keeper would organise a defence.
- Agility: In Dodgeball it's imperative to be quick around the area, much like goalkeeping, whether it is saving a shot or coming off the line quickly to gather up a through ball. This game will help develop being able to change direction quickly.
- Distribution: Different types of throws, like those used in a match, should be used - for example: the javelin, or the overarm throw. Aiming at an opponent is just like aiming at a team member, it has to be accurate and precise.
- Concentration: Keepers need to keep their eyes on the ball at all times like goalkeeping.

Typical Setup

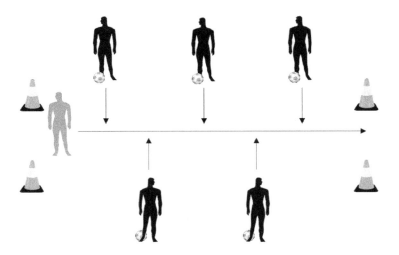

Circuit Training

Explanation

The idea of circuit training is to give goalkeepers a variety of small drills and exercises that will benefit their performance. Exercises like skipping, reaction work, speed and intensity work with balls, will enable goalkeepers to work on their all-round game and fitness.

Have as many different stations as you need to meet the group's requirements as well as any other exercises. Possibly hurdles, speed ladders or resistance methods.

Areas worked

With circuit training exercises, the focus will be on:

- Footwork
- Speed
- Intensity of practice
- Handling
- Varying exercises

Typical Setup

Each exercise will last for thirty seconds to a minute before moving on to the next. There will be two or three sets done depending on the physical state of the goalkeepers or time constraints.

1. Skipping.

2. Side to side diving saves. The GK sits down and saves the ball from a sitting position.

3. Rest and recovery period.

4. Cone reaction work. The GK has various cones spaced out around them, when a colour is called they will touch/dive on it then return to a standing start position.

5. Jumping and agility work.

- 10 x right leg hops
- 10 x left legs hope
- 10 x tuck jumps
- 10 x star jumps

6. Rest and recovery period.

Goalkeeper's Volleyball

Explanation

Using a volleyball or badminton net - goalkeepers should be separated into two teams. If a net is not available, then cones are an adequate alternative.

The aim of the game is to land the ball in the opponent's half, with the ball touching the floor in the designated area.

To restart play a serve is taken which is an underarm throw or drop kick from the back of the court. No 'lets' will be played and if the serve is out, hits the net, or doesn't reach the other half court - the opposing team gains control of the ball. Teams can score on their own serves or the opposing team's serve. Any body part can be used throughout the game, although catching is not allowed. A minimum number of passes between a team will be another progression along with a time limit to get the ball back over the net.

Different variations can be put in place such as:

- Every team member must touch the ball
- You can only score off your team's service game
- Different sizes and types of ball can be used
- Target scoring areas put around the pitch for punch or kick accuracy

Areas Worked

- Handling
- Communication
- Team organisation
- Decision making
- Game awareness

Potential Coaching Points

- Not stretching for the ball – control the body, move into line, and play back over
- Strong wrists and hands
- Timing of jumps and movement patterns

Game Starting Positions

- Coach plays the ball into the area
- Teams serve back in, after a point

Typical Setup

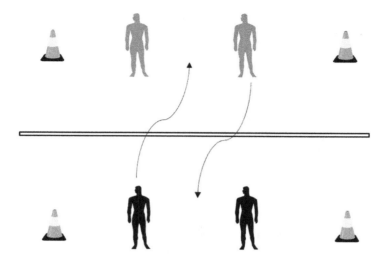

Goalkeeper's Tennis

Explanation

Different types of ball should be used with the objective of throwing, then passing, the ball through the coned goals. Different coloured goals are created with different coloured cones. Each goal will offer a varying number of points if scored through.

Two teams are needed, one either side of the dividing line. Each team has to stay in their half so collecting rebounds and recovery saves/recovery lines will be important. As in a football match the goalkeeper will have six seconds with the ball in their hands.

The game can be restarted by the coach or a sideline ball from where the ball went out. If the coach (standing on the sideline) scores a goal against a team - they will be deducted a point. Usually because of obvious poor positional play.

The winning team will be whichever team scores a certain amount of points first, or whichever team has accumulated the most points in an allotted time.

Areas Worked

- Distribution techniques (short/long passes, different types of throws)
- Basic handling techniques
- Diving saves
- Positional play
- Communication and organisation
- Concentration

There are also some variations to the game:

- Different balls
- Points for good play
- Specific methods of distribution, for example only using one type of throw
- Make one team's area smaller than the other team's and see how this affects positioning and tactics

Potential Coaching Points

- Changing position when the balls move (side to side, advance or drop)
- Saving the ball back into play (dangerous areas)
- Not committing too early on dives or other movements

Game Starting Positions

- From Coach
- Player who's scored against

Typical Setup

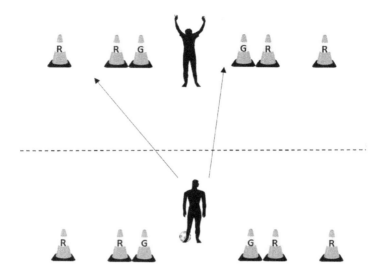

Goalkeeper's Tennis (No Hands)

Explanation

The same principles as volleyball should be used but the net will be considerably lower (or a coned substitute). The goalkeepers will only be allowed to use their feet and are limited in the number of touches they have (depending on what rules are used). To score a point, you have to bounce the ball on the opponent's side.

All serves will take place in the serving area; this will be a drop kick into the opponent's area. Two small games of this should be done with players in designated teams but split into equal numbers if possible. The games will be the best of three sets with each set being the first team to 11 points; if the scores are tied at 10-10, then each team will have to win by two clear points.

For progression, target areas can put around the pitch for extra scoring points. Also if the group is advanced, or you want to challenge them, then say that every player on the team needs to touch the ball before it goes back over the net, or that keepers need to use their weaker feet.

Areas Worked

- First touch
- Ball judgement
- Pass weight and accuracy

Potential Coaching Points

- Too soft or too firm passes
- Stretching for the ball
- Not being on toes ready to receive
- Changing position in relation to the ball

Game Starting Positions

- Coach starts by playing the ball in
- Team starts with a serve into play

Typical Setup

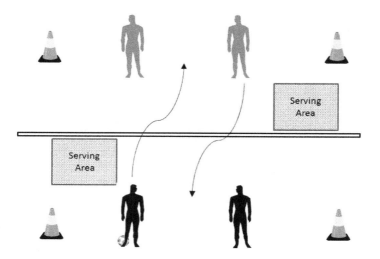

Keeper Combat

Explanation

This game is just the same as a normal small sided football practice except the goalkeeper can pick the ball up and use their hands to pass and score. All players can move anywhere on the pitch.

The rules that can be enforced are:

- Six seconds with ball in hand
- You can bounce, kick up, and punch the ball
- Any team who hits the ball outside the grid loses possession
- After a goal is scored the team who was scored against restarts with the ball or (for a changeup) the team who scores keeps possession
- No rugby-style tackling
- The ball can be run with for two seconds

Like a lot of the games here, the rules can be tweaked at your discretion.

Areas Worked

- Decision making
- General motor skills (jumping, catching, kicking, etc.)
- Co-ordination (using different balls; i.e. tennis balls, rugby balls, or futsal balls)
- Communication and organisation

To break up the game, a traditional small sided game can be played with all the goalkeepers acting as outfield players to enhance their game understanding, and ability with their feet.

Potential Coaching Points

- Not moving in accordance with the ball
- Committing too early (especially on a small pitch)
- Players making themselves big on reaction saves
- Commitment to saving the ball

Game Starting Positions

- Coach starts with a shot, high ball, or pass to either team
- Team who didn't touch last touch the ball, before it went out of play, starts on the sideline

Typical Setup

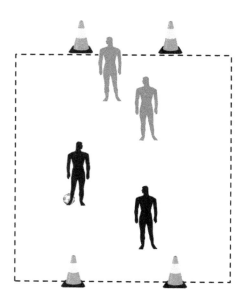

Basket-Keeper

Explanation

The same format as Basketball. If you have an indoor or outdoor pitch available – great. If not - trade the basket for a goal or equivalent. Use your imagination. I've used players as a target to catch the ball instead of a basket before!

Areas Worked

- General handling
- Quick dynamic movements
- Jumping
- Communication
- Organisation
- Decision making
- Footwork

Once again you can add in relevant rules such as six seconds on the ball, and having everyone touch the ball - so every goalkeeper will get the chance to use their skills.

Typical Setup

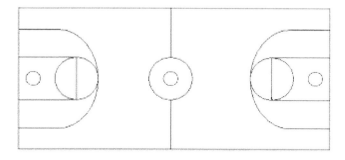

Bench-ball

Explanation

There are two teams with one member of each team on the opposite bench to their team. If you don't have a bench, use a coned off area. The objective is to get the ball to the person on the bench and whoever does this will join the person already on the bench. The team that gets all their team members on the bench first will be the winner. If a bench isn't used the elevated advantage is lost – so if using a coned area a greater emphasis would be placed on jump height and timing.

The opposition team can gain control of the ball by intercepting it. When a team gets a person on the bench, the ball will go to the other team. If the ball goes out of bounds, the team who didn't touch it last will get the ball. Again different balls can be used and the six-second law can be enforced so goalkeepers get into good habits with the ball in their hands. This exercise gets goalkeepers used to timing their jumps off both legs - both to intercept and to catch the ball above the opposition.

Areas Worked

- Jumping
- General handling
- Decision making
- Team organisation

Potential Coaching Points

- Timing of the jump
- Adaptable movements in accordance with the ball
- The decision of punch or catch

Game Starting Positions

- Coach plays the ball into the area to restart at any point

Typical Setup

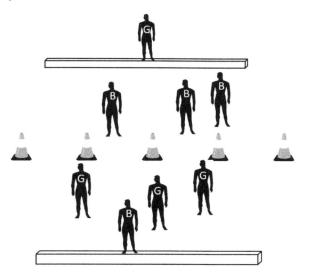

Face and Dive

Explanation

This game is a very good prescribed warm-up exercise and will get a goalkeeper psychologically sharp and physically ready for a session.

It can be done with one or two goalkeepers in a grid, as shown below.

The coach will call a colour and a way to dive, for example, "BLUE, RIGHT". The goalkeeper will have to face the coloured goal the coach has called, and then dive in the called direction pretending to save a type of shot. This could be low or high and without a ball the goalkeeper can work through his or her technique slowly.

A ball will be located in each goal so that goalkeepers have a target to fix their eyes on when facing the goal. Once a diving save has been made, each keeper will recover quickly into an upright and set position - ready for the next instruction from the coach.

This exercise can also be done with servers at each goal working the goalkeeper in the grid. This will work both the goalkeeper and the server psychologically as the servers will also have to concentrate and respond appropriately to the coach's call to produce the correct serve.

If there is a group of six, have the goalkeeper *not* in the exercise doing ball familiarity exercises and keep swapping the servers and the working goalkeeper.

Areas Worked

- Diving technique
- Concentration and attention
- Reaction time

Typical Setup

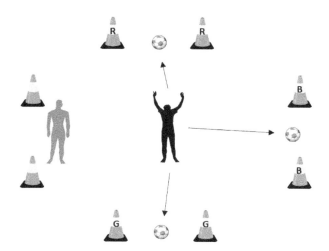

Follow the Keeper

Explanation

Again this is a good warm up exercise whilst working on a technique. The working goalkeepers will line up in single file and start to jog around the playing area. When "GO" is shouted from the coach, or server, the goalkeeper at the front of the line will advance from the line, get set, and then receive a certain save. They will then throw the ball back to the server and jog back to the end of the line. When they have completed this action, the next goalkeeper will make a save, and so on.

Typical Setup

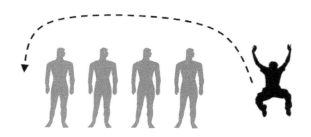

Lines

Explanation

The aim of the game is to work on diving technique when saving low shots, making collapse saves and high-handed saves.

The goalkeepers will be lined up facing one working goalkeeper, who will then proceed to work along the line receiving a diving save (the direction is up to the server) all the way along, and then on the way back.

For the coach, the key thing is to get the working goalkeeper to stand up quickly and set in line with the next ball. Because the working goalkeeper doesn't know which direction the ball is going, they must not anticipate and gamble.

Typical Setup

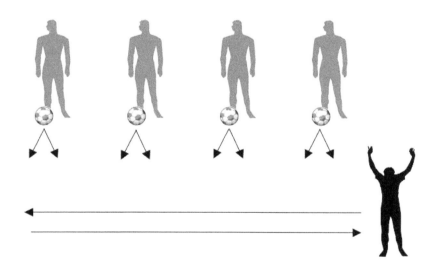

Piggy in the Middle

Explanation

The goalkeeper at either end must get the ball over to the goalkeeper at the opposite end, using one method of distribution at a time. For example, it could be ground kicking a stationary ball, throwing, or a moving ball where a lay-off would be provided by the goalkeeper in the middle. The goalkeeper in the middle will have a designated area to stay in.

The goalkeeper in the middle will try and stop the ball; if they succeed, they will get one point. If the goalkeeper at either end gets the ball over to the opposite side, this is again worth one point. The winner will be the goalkeeper with the most points once everyone has been in each position. For progressions, you could change the position of the middle goalkeeper's area plus increase or decrease the size of the grid.

Areas Worked

- Distribution methods
- Handling and judgement (middle goalkeeper)
- First touch and control (end goalkeepers)
- Accuracy and type of passes

Potential Coaching Points

- The timing of movements
- Decision on when to move, in accordance with the ball
- How the middle goalkeeper best keeps the ball out of the net

Game Starting Positions

- Coach plays the ball to either end player
- Goalkeeper in the middle starts with the ball, plays to either end player (underarm roll or pass), and has to react off their first touch

Typical Setup

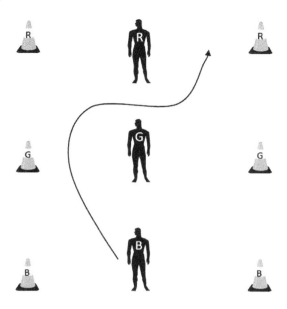

Back Ball/Knees

Explanation

The aim of the game is for the designated goalkeeper, with any kind of ball, to touch their opponents on the middle of the back with their ball. This will promote staying 'face on' to the ball at all times. Alternatively, goalkeepers can try and touch each other on the knees, both front and back. This has been found to prompt goalkeepers into getting into a lower stance with their hands down low, much like facing a 1v1, or a close range shot. This will get keepers into good habits when faced with this situation in a match.

Areas Worked

- Concentration/awareness
- Different set positions
- Quick feet

Typical Setup

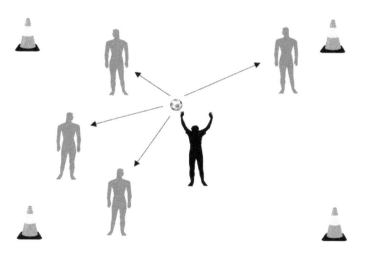

Further progressions are that a ball can be added for the team to pass or throw around while the goalkeeper who is 'in the middle' is trying to go about his job. Another progression sees each goalkeeper having a ball and trying to 'tag' each other on the back or knees.

Keeper's Union

Explanation

This mini-game is a great way to finish off any session! The group is divided into two sides with one occupying each half. The idea is to try and score as many goals as possible in a set time. This can be done by whatever means necessary as long as each team stays in their own half. The goalkeepers on each team can pass between themselves if they desire (changing the angles and distances) or they can go straight for goal once they produce a save. A group of balls will be placed by either goal to ensure a quick turnaround with each team taking alternate shots.

To keep things interesting you can introduce uneven teams (2v4) or change the distance in one half by making it shorter or longer.

Areas Worked

- Decision making
- Shot stopping (parrying, deflecting and catching)
- Concentration
- Appropriate positioning
- Reactions

Potential Coaching Points

- Moving into line with the ball
- Staying square onto the ball
- Can the goalkeeper make an early decision on how to deal with the ball
- Commitment to wanting to keep the ball out

Game Starting Positions

- Coach takes a shot at either team
- Coach plays a pass into a team who controls and shoots
- Coach plays a high ball into either area
- One team starts with the ball, and plays it over to the other team who then start the game after their first touch

Typical Setup

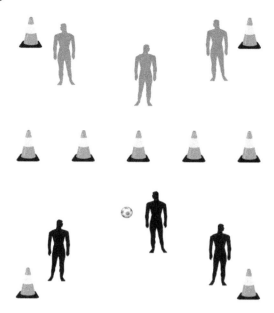

Alternative Setups

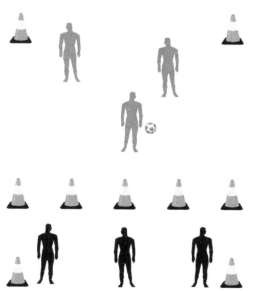

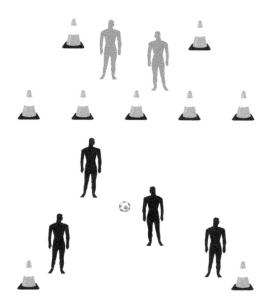

The winning team is the one that scores the most goals in the time allowed. Alternatively, the winning team could be the one that produces the most saves, it's up to you!

Mini Match

Explanation

Mini Match is similar to "Quick Attack" where a small group is located in an end grid performing an exercise such as passing, saving, etc.

When the coach calls two names or numbers (if players are numbered up), the keepers must advance together towards the two goals and try to score past either of the goalkeepers.

These two 'attackers' can pass between themselves and have a maximum of six seconds to have an attempt on goal. Rounds of seven will be carried out, and the goalkeeper with the least goals conceded will be the winner. Two different goalkeepers will be selected to go in goal, and this process will continue until everyone has had a spell in goal.

Areas Worked

- Decision making
- Shot stopping (parrying, deflecting and catching)
- Anticipation
- Positioning in relation to the ball

Potential Coaching Points

- Does the goalkeeper take up an appropriate position in relation to the ball
- Are they on the front foot when the ball is being played around in the grid
- Handling techniques
- Skilful saves
- Being hard to beat

Game Starting Positions

- Game will always start with the players in the grid passing the ball around

Typical Setup

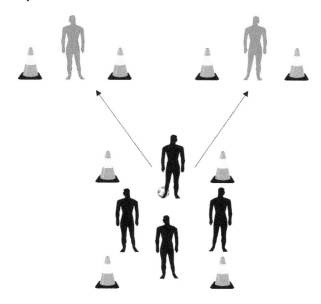

A progression of this game can be where there is one attacker and one defender from the grid, thus adding a communication and organisational element to the game. Also, only one goal might be used so the working goalkeeper has a chance to work closely with one defender. However, this would work better with a smaller group so each goalkeeper gets more turns being in goal and can practice the skills mentioned earlier.

Warm Up Goals

Explanation

A great exercise if you have four+ goalkeepers. The working goalkeepers will start in the middle of all the mini-goals and move into any goal they choose, produce a save (one that has been stated by the coach before the start or randomly) and then move onto any other goal they choose. In between saves they should be performing dynamic stretches and movements relevant to the upcoming sessions.

The servers will switch with the working goalkeepers after two minutes (for example), and this process will continue.

Areas Worked

- Cup, W, or Scoop
- Low handed dive
- High handed dive
- High ball
- Pass into left or right foot
- Control volley back to server
- Two diving saves (1 each side or 2 consecutive)
- Dynamic stretches and movements

Typical Setup

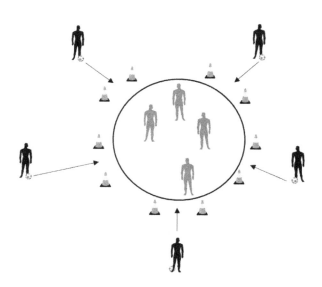

Touch Rugby

Explanation

Each team attacks an end trying to place a Rugby ball down on the ground behind an end line. If anyone is touched during the game whilst holding the ball, they must place the ball on the ground and pass the ball back between their legs to another team member.

The ball is not allowed to go forward; if this occurs the ball will be turned over. A ball going out of play will result in the ball being given to the team who was not in possession last. The ball is also not allowed to be kicked at any point.

The winning team at the end of the allotted time will be the one with the most points.

Areas Worked

- Basic handling
- Quick, explosive footwork
- Communication
- Decision making
- General motor skills

Potential Coaching Points

- The timing of movements
- Acceleration with the ball (speed)
- Are the goalkeeper's feet quick when moving
- Can the goalkeepers mirror movements and get into line with the ball

Game Starting Positions

- Either team starts with the ball
- One team plays the ball to the other, and the game begins
- Coach plays a high ball in that's contested between both teams

Typical Setup

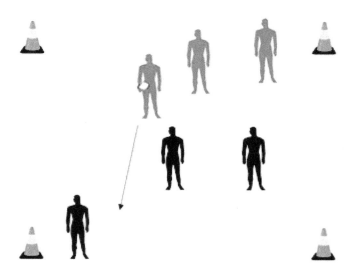

Keeping with the Hands

Explanation

On a small pitch (depending on numbers) goalkeepers will be placed in even teams attacking the opposite goal. The only difference between this game and a standard small sided game is that tackling is done with the hands. When the ball is won the goalkeeper must place the ball at their feet and try to score in the opposition's goal.

Each team will have a designated goalkeeper in their goal that rotates at the coach's discretion, or players can move freely wherever they please. Sideline and goal kicks are taken with the hands using an underarm roll. The team with the most goals wins, or alternatively the team that makes the most clean 1v1 takes will win.

Areas Worked

- 1v1 situations
- Building confidence and timing
- Decision making

Potential Coaching Points

- Not committing
- Staying big and delaying the attacker
- Moving in accordance with the ball
- Can the goalkeepers use controlled aggression

Game Starting Positions

- Coach starts with the ball and plays to one of the teams (varying heights)
- Either team starts with the ball
- If scored against, that teams starts with the ball
- Side-line balls start with the team who did not touch it last

Typical Setup

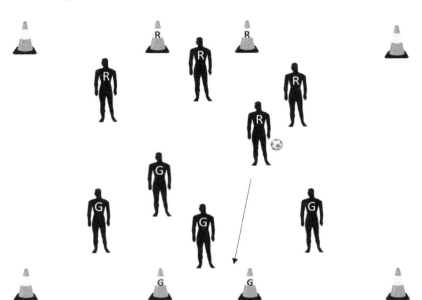

Games-Based Handling and Shot Stopping

Handling and Shot Stopping will be the main focus of the games in this section although other areas of goalkeeping will be worked on throughout. These will be listed in the 'Areas Worked' sections.

Four Goal Game

Explanation

The aim of the game is to score as many goals in the opposition's goal(s) as possible. One goal scored equals one point. The goalkeeping group will be divided into four teams each defending a coloured goal. If you have a team of four players, then one goal per keeper can be used. If you have an odd number of players, assign two goals to individual players.

You score by throwing or passing the ball on the floor, into the goal, although it may be preferable to choose just one method at a time to avoid confusion. Whoever concedes a goal will restart with the ball between their goals. You may handle the ball anywhere on the pitch. A good way to start the practice is to say that a goal can only be scored by dribbling past the goalkeeper – this way the participants will get a feel for the environment.

If the ball goes out of play, then the ball will go back to the coach or the person who retrieves the ball. Double points can be scored at the coach's discretion; for example, if he asks for a certain type of throw to be used. If the grid is made small then reaction saves can be worked on; when a goalkeeper gains control of the ball in such a small area they should be told to shoot early and from close range.

Different types and sizes of ball can be used to keep the goalkeepers on their toes. Tennis balls are good to use for this game because the emphasis will be very much on assured handling and control.

Many or fewer goals can be used depending on the number of goalkeepers or equipment available.

Areas Worked

- Basic handling techniques
- Positioning
- Short distribution

- Reactions
- Concentration

Potential Coaching Points

- Reaction saves
- Positioning
- Reaction off the attackers' first touch
- Not committing on 1v1s
- Recovery saves after initial contact
- Concentration when ball is in play

Game Starting Positions

- Coach plays to one of the goalkeepers who starts the game
- Coach shoots at any of the goalkeepers
- Coach plays a high ball to one of the goalkeepers
- Coach plays the ball into the middle for a contest
- Coach plays a pass to one goalkeeper, who then has to pass to another goalkeeper with the game starting off their touch

Typical Setup

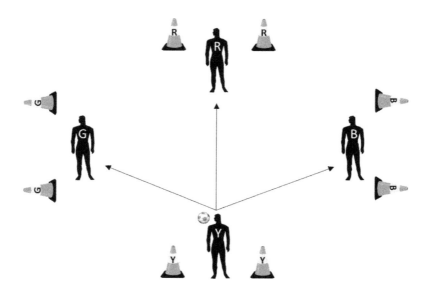

Triangle Goal Game

Explanation

The coach will call a coloured goal for the goalkeeper to move into – to save a shot. When a save is completed the same process will be repeated until the working goalkeeper's turn is over; this could be any number of shots depending on the intensity of the exercise and the numbers the coach wants to work with. Also, to keep practice realistic (especially for older goalkeepers) keep the service varied.

Different sized balls can be used once again, so the goalkeeper has to adjust their technique accordingly.

Along with coloured cones, the coach could decide to rename the colours with things associated to that colour, for example, in the below diagram the blue goal could be called 'sea', the green could be 'grass', and the yellow could be 'sun'.

As another progression the coach could name the goals as things that are *not* associated with that colour to really test the goalkeeper's thinking and decision making skills; for example the blue goal could be called 'car', the green could be 'train', and the yellow could be 'plane'.

This game can also be set up with more than three goals, with the same principles and setup used. Remember to keep this game short and sharp – with no more than a minute of action. For younger keepers, you might want to slow the game down to focus on particular technical coaching points.

Areas Worked

- Reactions
- Basic handling techniques
- Low/high diving save
- Short explosive movements

Typical Setup

Double Team

Explanation

There are three teams with varying numbers of team members depending on the group's size. Two team members is a good size, but three or four could also be used.

Two teams go into the end goals with the team 'in the middle' being the main shot stopping workers.

An end team will take a shot from their goal line and try to score against the middle goalkeepers; if they do so, they will receive a point. If they also manage to score against the team in the opposite goal they will receive three points.

The middle goalkeepers will receive one point if they save the shot and parry it outside the grid into a safe area. If they keep hold of the ball before it goes out, then they will get three points. Any recovery saves after an initial save will count as well.

The coach or goalkeepers can decide the target time in the middle and how far apart the goals are. If an aim is to work on reaction saves then bring the goals closer together.

The two end goals can be a real goal net with the middle goal being cones. If cones are used then head height rules will apply in the middle. If cones are only used then head height (or a pre-determined height) should apply to all goals.

The team with the most points after each team has been in the middle will be the winner.

Areas Worked

- Shot stopping/parrying/deflecting
- Reaction saves
- Recovery saves
- Top hand saves
- Kicking
- Concentration

Potential Coaching Points

- Are the goalkeepers' saves effective
- Positioning in relation to the ball
- Reaction off the attackers' first touch

- Concentration when team at the opposite end has the ball
- Can the middle goalkeeper be brave and aggressive
- Stay chest on to the ball in middle

Game Starting Positions

- Coach plays to one of the end teams for a shot
- Coach shoots at one of the end teams who then start with a shot
- Coach plays a high ball to the end teams; they claim and then take a shot
- Coach plays a pass to middle goalkeepers who then pass to end goalkeepers, reacting off their touch

Typical Setup

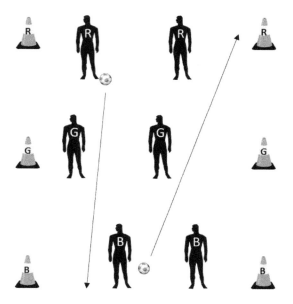

Quick Attack

Explanation

The aim for the goalkeeper in this game is to get into the correct position to save an oncoming shot. The goalkeeper should work on getting into line with the ball and set when the attackers are preparing to shoot.

The game works with the non-working goalkeepers in a grid either passing the ball between themselves or performing handling exercises (for example, scoop saves or low handed saves). When the coach calls a colour, the working goalkeeper in the goal area will touch that cone and move into position in relation to the ball and the middle of the goal - ready to save a shot.

When the colour is called the goalkeeper with the ball in the grid will become an attacker and when the working goalkeeper is in position will have four seconds to score a goal. This can also be done without the coloured cones, perhaps making the game more realistic, as the goalkeeper does not come out of position to start with.

The position of the shooting line can be altered depending on what the session topic is. 1v1s can be worked on with the line being close to the goal, or long range shot stopping can be attempted with the shooting line moved far back.

The working goalkeeper will be rotated with the number of goals conceded recorded. The goalkeeper with the lowest number will be the winner.

Areas Worked

- Positioning
- Shot stopping
- Parrying into safe areas

Potential Coaching Points

- Re-adjustment of position
- Can the goalkeeper take up an effective position
- Being set and balanced upon impact of the ball

Game Starting Positions

- Game always starts from the grid

Typical Setup

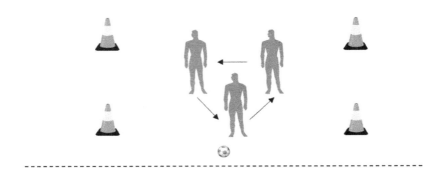

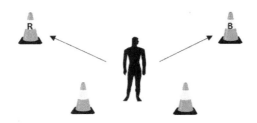

The shooting line can vary as discussed above.

The Circle of Saves

Explanation

There will be one goalkeeper in the middle and the others in a circle formation around him or her. The working goalkeeper will go around the circle either clockwise or anti-clockwise making different kinds of saves depending on the session topic (or for a warm up, just basic handling such as the scoop or cup).

The servers on the outside can be stationary or moving, and the distance away from the working goalkeeper is up to the coach or the goalkeeper.

After a few rotations of the circle, the working goalkeeper will swap with another. On any keeper's subsequent turn the direction they work in should be reversed.

Areas Worked

- Basic handling techniques
- Recovery saves

Typical Setup

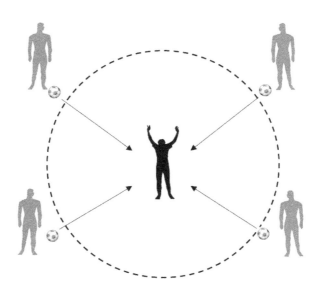

Team Keeper

Explanation

Each goalkeeper will start in a goal but is free to move around the pitch and use their hands in the whole area. However, they are not allowed behind their goal into the area 'in-between the goals'. This area will be cordoned off by cones in the middle.

The outfield players will be aiming to score, and if they do so they will get a point. They will be passing between themselves, changing angles and distances, but keeping the tempo high at match pace. If the goalkeepers claim the ball or make a save that goes outside the grid (or is of high enough quality to merit a point) then they will gain one point.

The ball is only dead when the goalkeeper has two hands on the ball, or the ball leaves the playing area. If a goal is scored, for example, and the ball is kept in the playing area - the game continues.

If any goalkeeper enters the coned off area, they will be deducted a point. It's up to the coach to determine what points total will be the target for both teams.

The example setup has three goals and five outfield players but this can be adapted to more goals if there are more participants. Alternatively, the coach can overload the attackers to make it harder for the goalkeepers.

Areas Worked

- Set position
- Reaction saves
- Concentration
- Appropriate positioning
- Footwork

Potential Coaching Points

- Does the goalkeeper take up appropriate positions in relation to the ball
- Are they committed to making saves
- Can they claim the ball where possible
- Does the goalkeeper chase the ball, or prove too eager to commit at the outfield players' feet

Game Starting Positions

- Coach plays the ball to an outfield player
- Coach plays the ball to a goalkeeper who then passes to an outfield player – having to react off their first touch
- Outfield players play a number of passes to each other before the game is live
- First pass can be free between outfield players

Typical Setup

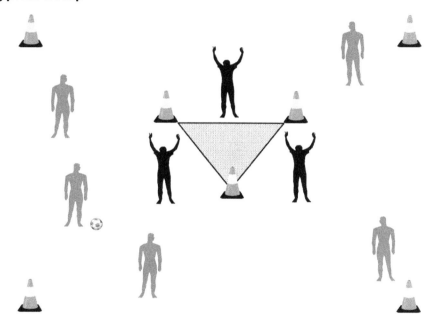

Own Goal

Explanation

There are two teams, each of which has the objective of eliminating all members of the opposing team. This is done by scoring a goal against a goalkeeper which results in them losing a life; all players start with three lives, for example. The setup is shown with six goalkeepers but more or fewer goals can be added alongside different goal positions.

Each goalkeeper will have an allocated goal which they have to defend. However they are allowed to move freely around their own side of the pitch.

Shots will be taken using the feet or the hands depending on the session, but not both in the same game. Goalkeepers can't move with the ball in hand but may throw to a team member. Passing may be done within any team to change angles and shot distances.

If a goal is scored, the beaten goalkeeper will start with the ball, but if the goal means a keeper is eliminated then the attacking team will have the ball back. When out of bounds the coach will restart the game.

The goal height will be up to the coach depending on the age, ability, and equipment available but the head height rule is a good way to go to clear up any confusion.

The winning team will have eliminated all opponents.

Areas Worked

- Decision making
- Concentration
- Shot stopping
- Reactions

Potential Coaching Points

- Can the goalkeepers make reaction saves
- Are keepers set in, and around, their goal area
- Does the goalkeeper attack the line or stay on the goal line
- Head and hands forward

Game Starting Positions

- Coach plays a high ball to either team – they then place the ball down and play
- One team plays to the other who then look to attack
- Coach takes a shot at a particular goalkeeper from varying positions outside the playing area

Example Setup

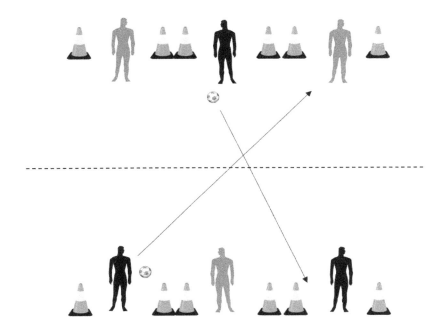

Zones

Explanation

This game can be played on a number-of-lives basis or by a simple scoring system (one goal scored equates to one point). The position of the goals can change; for example, on an angle, close to the line, or further away to vary the type of shots being received. Goalkeepers must stay in their zone. If they enter the opposing zones, they will either be deducted a point/goal or give one to the other team. The game can work on the basis of two teams (each side of the dividing lines) or alternatively each keeper against each other.

The rules are the same as "Own Goal" but a target score should be set. Have every goalkeeper rotating zones so they get a taste of new angles and situations.

Areas Worked

- Decision making
- Concentration
- Shot stopping
- Reactions
- Teamwork (if the game is setup as one team vs another)

Potential Coaching Points

- Can the goalkeepers make reaction saves
- Is the goalkeeper in position in relation to the ball
- Is the keeper set in, and around, their goal area
- Does the goalkeeper attack the line or stay on the goal line
- Head and hands forward

Game Starting Positions

- Coach plays a high ball into either team – they then place the ball down and play
- One team plays to the other who then look to attack
- Coach takes a shot at a particular goalkeeper from varying positions outside the playing area

Example Setup

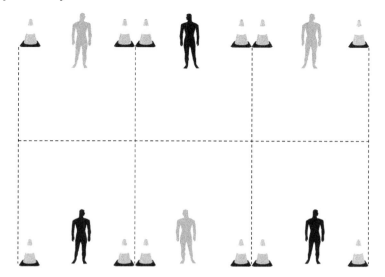

Outnumbered

Explanation

The idea with "Outnumbered" is that there are players/servers (each with a ball) located around a designated area, each of whom takes various shots at the working goalkeeper.

When the shot is saved, then the goalkeeper must throw the ball back to the server in order for the game to be continuous (and to practice distribution after claiming a ball).

The outside servers can be stationary or moving. These players will be defined as numbers, colours, animals, etc. to keep the goalkeeper alert. They will take a shot, one at a time.

This game can also be done in pairs with goalkeepers receiving alternate shots.

The serves can be along the floor, throws, or drop volleys depending on the goalkeepers – you might start with throwing for a warm up and then progress to moving balls.

Once again the distance and shape of the area can vary depending on the topic - a small area for reaction work, large for long range, or a circle so shot angles will change.

Areas Worked

- Reaction saves
- Getting into line with the shot
- Decision making

Example Setup

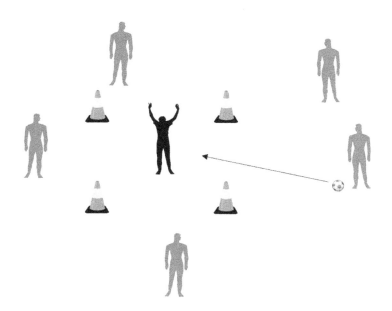

Multi-Goal

Explanation

There are three separate goals in the designated playing area that three goalkeepers have to defend. The attackers will be trying to score by working together to beat the goalkeepers. Play starts from the coach or a floating player outside the playing area; they may play the ball in wherever they wish to vary the angles and types of play.

Goalkeepers score a point for a save and attackers for a goal scored. When one team reaches a certain number of points, the goalkeepers will switch so everyone has a turn in goal. The positions of each goal can be changed to create alternative scenarios and to mix the play up. This would include perhaps placing a defender within the practice.

Something that works well is if the coach starts with the ball at their feet and shifts the ball out, in any direction, such that goalkeepers will have to change their position in the goal in accordance to the position of the ball. Here you can work on the front foot start, and re-positioning, after a phase of play.

Areas Worked

- Shot stopping
- Positioning
- 1v1 situations
- Crossing

Potential Coaching Points

- Are the goalkeepers on the front foot
- Do the goalkeepers shift into line
- Appropriate handling techniques
- Desire and commitment to keep the ball out
- Only moving when the ball is not under the control of an outfield player

Game Starting Positions

- Coach plays a ball into the goalkeepers, who then distribute to an outfield player reacting off their first touch
- Coach plays the ball to the outfield players
- Coach varies their position outside the grid, and plays a ball to be contested by both the goalkeepers and outfield players
- Outfield players play a one-two with the goalkeepers, the game is live after the outfielders' touch

- An outfield player passes a ball to a goalkeeper, the goalkeeper then plays the ball to another outfield player, the ball is then live off their touch

Typical Setup

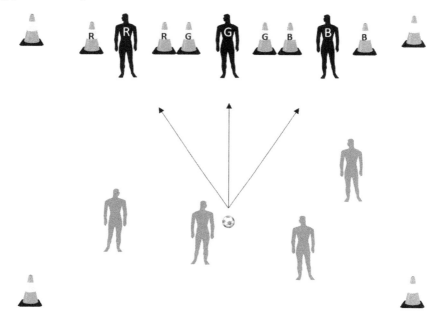

Get To The Next One!

Explanation

The goalkeeper will work his or her way through a series of goals. The servers must wait until the goalkeeper is set before shooting (or to keep the practice more realistic the goalkeeper will have to set based on the visual cues they receive from the shooter). The working goalkeeper will have to get to the next goal as quickly as possible. Once they have completed the set everyone will change positions and rotate. Although a speed orientated game, don't let the quality diminish.

Areas Worked

- Shot stopping
- Speed
- General agility
- Footwork
- Decision making

Example Setup

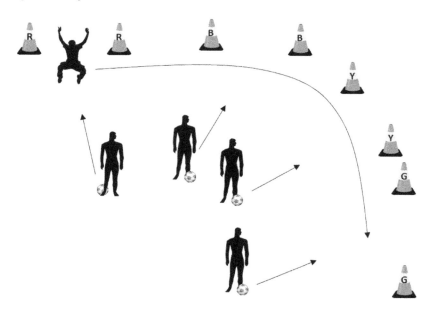

An alternative set up can be arranged so that, like the first set up, the goalkeeper has to get to the goals as quickly as possible. However this time the coach can call a specific goal the player has to get to. These goals can be defined by colours, numbers, player names, or trigger words to get the goalkeepers used to making quick split second decisions.

The working goalkeeper must return to the starting cone before the next shot.

Alternative Setup

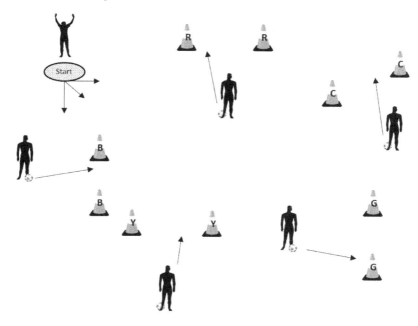

Backwards and Forwards

Explanation

In the example shown below, the goalkeeper will receive shots from all four servers at the first line of goals. He/she will then carry on receiving shots at the second line from the servers (over a longer distance). Once completed, the keeper will move onto the third line of goals. The working goalkeeper should receive a total of 12 shots from three different ranges.

This exercise can be done going backwards or forwards, hence the name.

The types of shots the goalkeeper can receive are varied but in a higher ability group they should all be diving shots working in either direction for varied practice.

For a progressive, competitive element, the aim will be to concede as few goals as possible - these shots should really test the goalkeeper.

Areas Worked

- Speed
- Agility
- Power
- Basic handling techniques

Example Setup

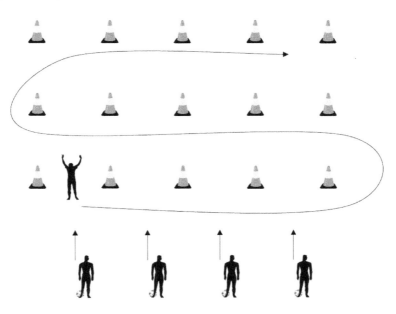

Goalie-Ball

Explanation

Goalie-Ball is a game that has been taken from blind sport and adapted for the world of conventional goalkeeping. It's a simple game where the ball must not go over a goal line following a shot from the opposing team. The teams will score points for a goal scored, and the winner will be the first team to a certain number of goals.

Shots can be taken with the hands or feet. Both methods can be used in the same game, or separately. When a goal is scored, the team who has conceded a point will have control of the ball. The ball is not allowed to be passed between the team so the goalkeeper who makes a save or pounces on a rebound must distribute the ball. Team zones can also be added to keep things fresh.

Areas Worked

- Distribution methods
- Shot stopping and handling

Potential Coaching Points

- Saving shapes on each shot
- Explosive, dynamic movements
- Moving up and down the line of the ball

Game Starting Positions

- Coach plays the ball to either team
- The ball is passed between each team; the coach will then show a coloured cone or shout a command. After this, the ball is live

Typical Setup

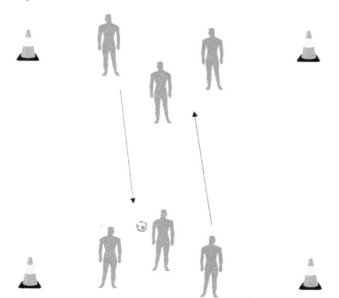

The Pit

Explanation

All the goalkeepers will start in 'The Pit' where they will pass a ball to each other using feet or hands, do ball rotations, or move around without a ball doing actions such as skipping and high fives.

Every goalkeeper will have a number. When this number is called they will advance into the goal and face two challenging shots; if they save both they will move to the winner's area, if not then they will go back to 'The Pit'. Depending on the group's size, the number of shots at each goalkeeper could be reduced to one.

At the end, there will be one goalkeeper left and they will have been left in 'The Pit'. The game could also continue by having an overall winner through the elimination of the losing goalkeeper every turn. Once there are two goalkeepers left in 'The Pit' at any one time they should both have the opportunity to go into sudden death for a fairer game.

Don't get stuck in THE PIT!

Areas Worked

- Decision making
- Quick thinking
- Shot stopping

Potential Coaching Points

- Watching the ball all the time
- Being set despite maybe being out of position
- Keeper reacting to their name being called
- Does the goalkeeper show quick, explosive movements
- Does the goalkeeper show desire to keep the ball out
- Watching for effective, maybe at times, unorthodox saves

Game Starting Positions

- Games always start in accordance with the explanation

Typical Setup

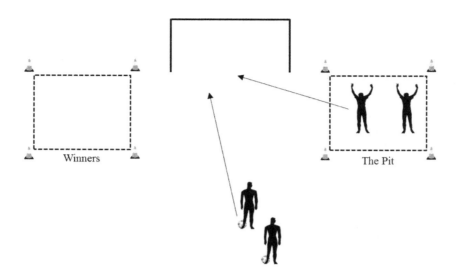

Winners

The Pit

Choices

Explanation

The working goalkeepers (labelled "1") will start by the starting cone and the coach will call a colour. The goalkeeper must then get to that coloured goal as quickly as they can. A time limit (depending on the ability of the goalkeepers) will be in place until the serving goalkeeper can shoot.

Teams of two keepers will be set up and turns will be alternated. The team with the least number of goals scored against them will be the winner.

Teams will rotate, For example, if there are six goalkeepers two would be working, two resting and keeping mobile, and two serving. More goals and bigger teams can be put in place if required. Each goalkeeper will receive the same number of shots; a good number would be five each - then they will move to the rest zone after working intensely.

Areas Worked

- Shot stopping
- Decision making
- Responding to verbal commands

Typical Setup

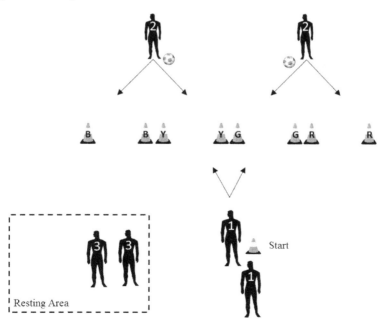

69

Back to Back

Explanation

The diagram shows two netted goals turned back to back and a small pitch created around the outside. The aim of "Back to Back" is for the players to score in either of these goals, and they can do this by playing the ball anywhere on the pitch. This could be over the goals, around the goals, etc.

The goalkeeper's job, as usual, is to stop the ball going into their goal.

Goalkeepers can work as a team against the attackers and score a point for a save with the attackers scoring one for a goal, or they can work against each other and the one that concedes the fewest goals in the allotted time will be the winner and get to stay on while the other goalkeeper is swapped.

If a goal is scored against a keeper, he/she can restart by kicking the ball onto the pitch wherever they want. If a ball goes over the sideline then the ball re-enters from that spot.

Players can move freely anywhere on the pitch, but the goalkeepers must stay in their respective goals. Outfield players, despite being goalkeepers, aren't allowed to use their hands.

Areas Worked

- Reaction saves
- Positioning
- Concentration

Potential Coaching Points

- Being big and brave
- Is the goalkeeper always on their toes, ready to move into line with the ball
- Being skilful and adaptable in keeping the ball out of the goal

Game Starting Positions

- Goalkeeper rolls a ball out to an outfield player (who cannot score against them)
- Coach plays the ball in, anywhere within the playing area
- Coach plays the ball to an outfielder who starts the play

Typical Setup

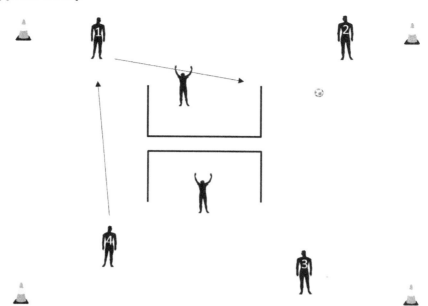

Inside Out

Explanation

All goalkeepers will be located around the main grid but outside the small coned-off grid. They will either pass or throw the ball between each other using a variety of different methods. While this is going on the coach in the blue coned-off grid will call a goalkeeper's name, and the keeper will have to get to the nearest blue cone, go around it, then produce a diving save. As the middle grid is a square, it represents four mini goals. As the game progresses, the coach can test the goalkeepers more and more by adapting the outside group's activities.

Areas Worked

- Concentration
- Dive technique
- Basic handling
- Speed (body and mind)
- Distribution methods (outside grid)

Typical Setup

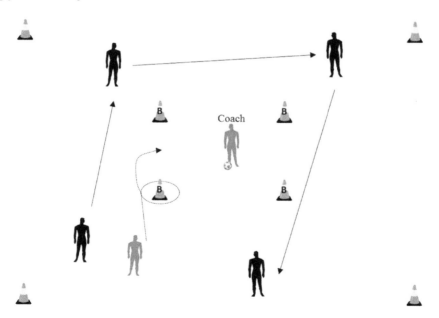

Testing the Angles

Explanation

When a goalkeeper has control of the ball (in this case the green goalkeeper), they can score in either of the other keepers' goals.

To start with, this exercise should be non-competitive, just working on angles, positioning, and basic handling using a drop volley service. But if used later on in a session it might be a game scenario with a point scored for each goal. Varied service can be used if desired but allow the goalkeepers no longer than six seconds with the ball before they must shoot.

Areas Worked

- Positioning
- Basic handling techniques
- Concentration

Setup

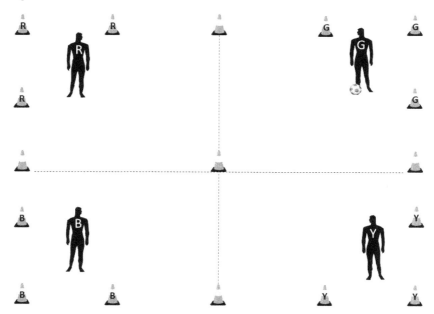

Boomerang

Explanation

Just like a Boomerang, it keeps coming back to you!

The game starts with one team receiving the ball; their objective is to score in one of the coloured goals shown. This is done by either taking a shot or dribbling into the goal depending on the topic. Alternatively, both plays can be done.

The attacking team are effectively outfield players so can't use their hands at any point. The goalkeeping team can use their hands anywhere. The attacking team can also pass the ball between each other.

Once a goal has been scored, or a save performed, that team then gains control of the ball. They then attack, and the game carries on back and forth, hence the name "Boomerang".

The attacking team can either attack straightaway, trying to catch the goalkeeping team off guard, or they can wait until they have recovered into their goal area, this is up to the coach.

After the allocated time or points target, the game is finished with a winner crowned. Red Goal = 1 point, Blue goal = 2 points, Yellow goal = 3 points.

Areas Worked

- Positioning
- Decision making
- Concentration
- Shot stopping
- Parrying/deflecting techniques

Potential Coaching Points

- Does the goalkeeper make appropriate decisions in terms of their saves, movements, and positioning
- Can the goalkeeper turn defence into attack quickly (transition of play)
- Keeping eyes on the ball at all times
- Being aware of when a pass is played, or when a shot is being taken

Game Starting Positions

- Coach plays a ball to be contested
- Coach plays the ball to either team

- Coach plays the ball to one team, who then passes the ball to the other – play is live off their first touch

Setup

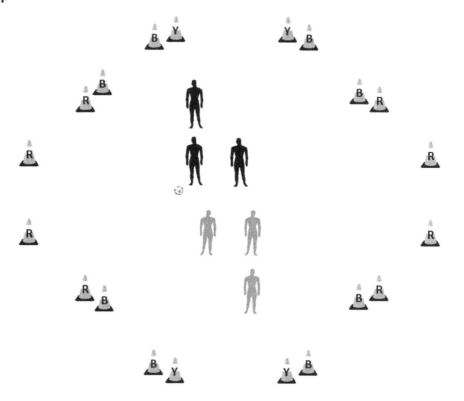

Alternative Setup

In this setup, there is only one goal area and the goalkeeping team stay in for a certain number of attacks. Once they have been completed, the sides will switch.

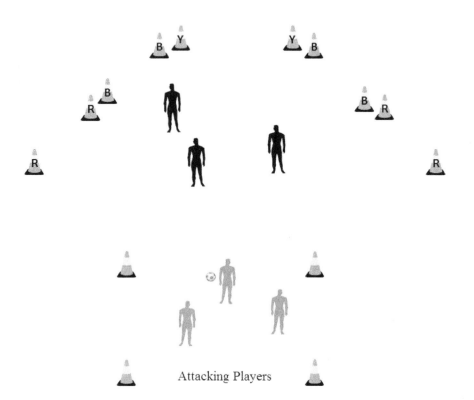

Attacking Players

Back 2 Goal

Explanation

With "Back 2 Goal" the working goalkeeper will always have their back to the next goal. The working goalkeeper will start facing a server (red in the below example) and when the game starts will proceed to the blue server first, then green, then back to red; this process will continue.

The keeper will have three seconds to get to the next goal before that server shoots at goal. This game can last for however long the coach desires, but for quality's sake - keep it to less than 30 seconds (equal to 10 shots).

The winner will be the goalkeeper who has conceded the fewest goals.

The servers can shoot from any angle or distance that the coach wants, in keeping with a session's theme.

Areas Worked

- Set position before shot
- Shot stopping
- Positioning
- Footwork (speed and agility)

Setup

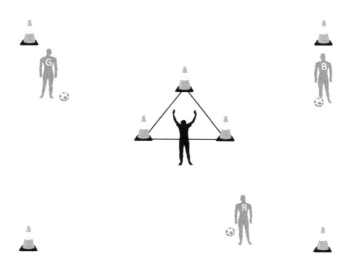

Stay in Control!

Explanation

This game involves the shooting goalkeeper (in the coned area) receiving a throw, volley or ground kick from one of the two serving GKs (in their respective circles) who will aim for their hands or feet. The shooting keeper will then either shoot at goal using a drop or half volley, or a shot off the floor if received with the feet.

The ball is continually recycled from these servers in the circles. The working goalkeeper will stay in the goal as long as he or she does not concede a goal. If a goal is conceded, then the working keeper moves to a serving position and one of servers becomes the shooter. Everyone continues to rotate when a goal is scored. The winner will be the goalkeeper who stays in the goal for the greatest number of shots.

A progression of this game is to change the position of the shooting grid or to make the grid smaller, so the servers have to be more accurate.

A great way to end a session!

Areas Worked

- Shot stopping
- Distribution methods

Potential Coaching Points

- Does the goalkeeper show commitment in wanting to stay in the goal
- The distribution accuracy of the goalkeeper in the circles
- Being set upon impact

Game Starting Positions

- Ball starts from the players in the circles, as mentioned above

Setup

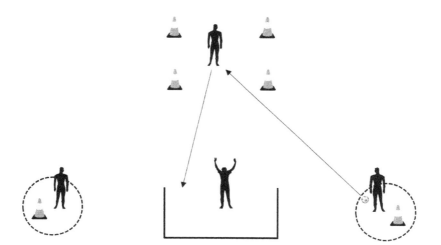

Beat the Goalie

Explanation

The game starts with the first goalkeeper receiving a shot on goal from either server. If they don't concede a goal, they will return to the back of either line. If they do concede a goal, they are out of the game.

The next designated goalkeeper will then move into the goal, position themselves, and receive a shot.

The servers will take alternate shots (raising their hand and calling) - giving the goalkeepers ample time to get set and into an appropriate position for the server's ball. The serves can vary from a stationary ball, to a shift-out-of-their-feet-and-strike, or even the servers playing a pass to each other and then shooting at goal.

The last goalkeeper not to concede a goal is declared the winner.

Areas Worked

- Shot stopping
- Positioning
- Moving into and down the line of the ball

Setup

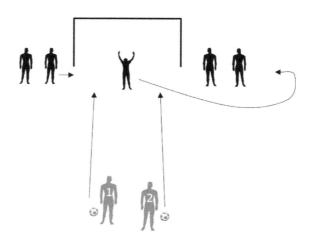

Ball Out!

Explanation

The working goalkeeper has to defend the blue coned goal while the outside players try to score through it. The goalkeeper has one minute to concede as few goals as possible. The players on the outside must shoot from outside the red area and are not allowed to pass to each other. If the goalkeeper claims the ball, they should play the ball back to the player who shot at them, but if they parry to save the shot - the nearest player should fetch the ball and then shoot.

Due to the quick-fire nature of this game, the outside players should be encouraged to shoot on sight and fetch balls quickly. To aid this, plenty of balls should be located around the playing area. After all the players have had a turn working as the goalkeeper, the one who has conceded the fewest goals is the winner. If a tie occurs, a sudden death 30 seconds can be operated.

Areas Worked

- Concentration
- Shot stopping
- Positioning
- Quickness (feet and mind)

Potential Coaching Points

- The goalkeeper committing – meaning they can't get back into position if the ball stays in play
- Deflecting the ball away from their goals
- Does the goalkeeper control their movements – staying composed and balanced throughout the game

Game Starting Positions

- Coach plays the ball to the attacking players from varying angles
- Coach plays the ball to the goalkeeper, who then passes to an outfield player to start the practice

Setup

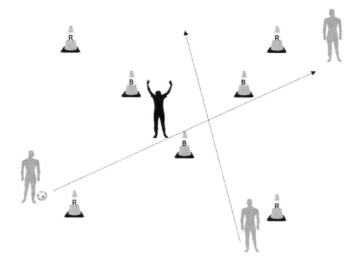

Games-Based Footwork and Distribution

Footwork and Distribution will be the main focus of the games in this section although other areas of goalkeeping will be worked on throughout. These will be listed in the 'Areas Worked' sections.

Obstacle Course

Explanation

An obstacle course can be made into a game where teams see how quickly they can complete the course (whilst keeping the correct technique of course). While one group is doing the obstacle course, another can be doing simple drills of possession passing or handling.

This exercise is mainly to work on goalkeeper fitness which is short, sharp bursts of movement. This includes jumping, quick foot movements, sharp changes in direction, and power jumps. You can add anything into the course - from using a ball throughout, to climbing over obstacles and footwork ladders. Keep the practices short (maximum a couple of minutes) and have goalkeepers walking before they perform a quicker more dynamic exercise – this will reflect the type of physical activity they have in a game. Make sure they work 360 degrees rather than just forwards, backwards and side to side.

Areas Worked

- Speed
- Agility
- Athleticism

Suggested Setup

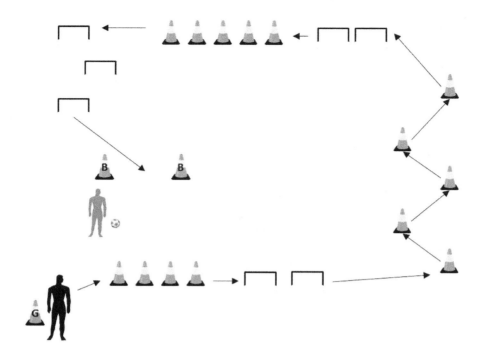

Slalom

Explanation

In the slalom run each goalkeeper will take it in turns to produce diving saves on a stationary ball on the ground; the aim is to work on diving technique for low balls and to get the body shape correct.

Once the keepers have progressed through the ball arrangement - footwork exercises will be done (any footwork can be done; e.g. hurdles, squats or lunges), the goalkeeper will then re-join the back of the line. After the front goalkeeper has done the first two sections of the slalom, the next keeper will go. The emphasis should be on correct techniques and not purely on speed.

Areas Worked

- Power
- Agility
- Speed
- Strength

Typical Setup

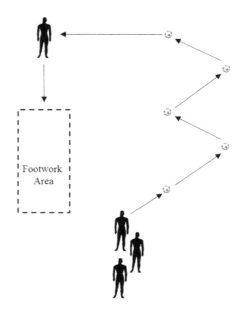

Moving Goal

Explanation

The aim of the Moving Goal game is to test a goalkeeper's footwork within a shot stopping setting. This exercise can also be used to build up power and strength through recovery saves.

The goalkeeper will receive a shot of the coach's choosing; if basic handling is being worked on then shots 'at' the goalkeeper but if diving, collapsed saves or high-handed saves are focused on - 'away' from the keeper. Serves can be tailored to fit the needs of the group. Keepers will then perform a series of footwork exercises in between receiving shots from the servers. This can be done with two working goalkeepers each starting opposite each other.

Areas Worked

- Power
- Strength
- Agility
- Basic handling

Typical Setup

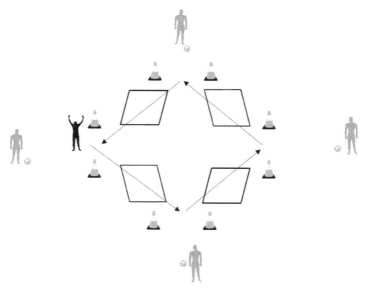

The 'Footlympics'

The aptly named "Footlympics" is designed to test the goalkeeper's footwork in a variety of situations that replicate match situations, for example being quick off the line, and using small steps to move into position.

All the games are timed in some way, and a points scoring system can be devised to determine who the overall winner is (e.g. 1st = 10 points, 2nd = 8 points, etc.).

Footlympics: Jumping Circuit

Explanation

The opening game is a test of speed and endurance with a small bit of throwing rolled into the equation.

Aim To roll as many balls through the gate, in one minute, as possible.

The participating goalkeeper will proceed from the start cone then:

- Do a two-footed jump over the first hurdle
- Do another two-footed jump over the left hurdle
- Retrieve a ball and repeat the process in the opposite direction
- Once over the final hurdle roll the ball through the gate cones to complete a set

Once this is done, the participant will then go to the station in front of them and then finally to the right-hand station. Once this is done, repeat the same order until the time is up.

Once the ball crosses the gate line - that will constitute a point; if cut off mid-set – the run will not count. The winner will be the goalkeeper who scores the most points (balls through the gate) in the allotted time.

It is worth putting at least two balls, if possible, by every station, or have someone collecting the balls behind the scoring gate.

Setup

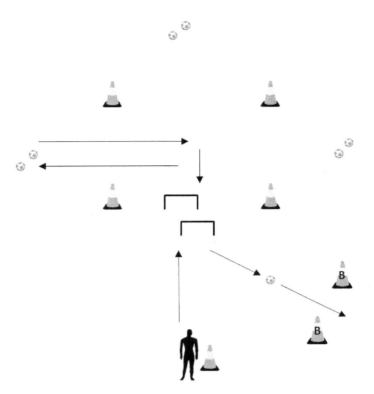

Footlympics: Get The Ball

Explanation

This event will test a goalkeeper's quick feet, and getting into line with the ball.

Aim To catch and return as many balls as possible in one minute.

The working goalkeeper will start at the blue cone and work his or her way around the grid using sidesteps and lateral running. When they are facing a server, they will get set, gain control of the ball, then return the ball back to that server. This will be done as many times as possible in one minute.

When a complete circuit has been done, the goalkeeper will touch the starting cone then proceed onto a new circuit.

Setup

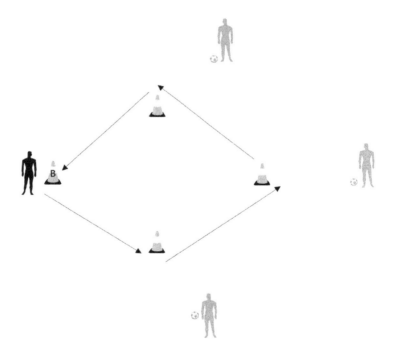

89

Footlympics: Coloured Feet

Explanation

The main focus of this game is to improve a goalkeeper's quick feet. "Coloured Feet" can have many variations, and adaptations can be easily moulded into more complex and intense periods of training.

Aim To score as many points as possible in one minute.

Within the setup, a point scoring system can be implemented to encourage quick and efficient footwork, an example of which will be explained below.

To start - the goalkeeper will receive a drop volley. Once claimed and thrown accurately back to the server the keeper will go and touch a coloured cone as quickly as they can, then proceed to re-enter the goal and receive another drop volley. This cycle will be completed as many times as possible in the allocated time, and the number of points scored will be added up to produce an overall score. The next goalkeeper will then have to beat that score in their run.

The points scoring system on the setup above has a green cone worth 1 point and a blue cone worth 2 points. It is a good idea to place the higher scoring cones further away, at an angle, or with an obstacle in front of them.

Other conditions can be placed on the game. For example, if the goalkeeper drops the ball they can have a point deducted, be made to start that turn again, receive a harder shot, or have to make the save from an irregular position, such as on their back.

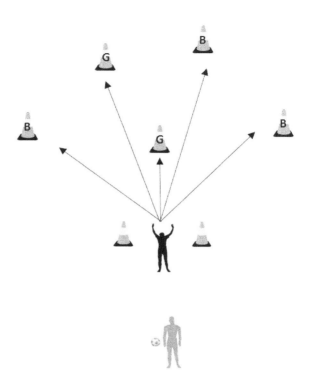

Alternative Setup

The alternative setup is designed to make the goalkeeper work forwards then backwards - as if they were recovering - to tip a shot over the bar or to get back into position.

The red cone in this setup is worth three points but has a hurdle in front requiring more effort to pick up the higher points. The goalkeeper will have to think of tactics and a strategy to gain the most points possible – so this is an exercise that also works them psychologically.

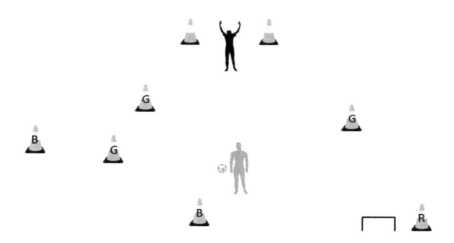

Footlympics: Andy Agility Meter

Explanation

The 4th event of the Footlympics will test the goalkeeper's speed and, as the name suggests, their agility.

Aim To complete the course in the quickest time possible.

The procedure is as follows:

- The goalkeeper will start by lying down with their hands behind the start line.
- The first part of the exercise will be to go in and out of the line of cones (facing at a 45-degree angle) changing from left to right as they go through.
- Once they have completed this, they will then work back through the poles any way they wish.
- The ladders are next, and both feet must be placed in each segment or this part will be done again (and the keepers head must be kept up, of course).
- Next, the goalkeeper will perform a collapse save and touch the cone with two hands before moving onto the next one. This will be done three times and is indicated by the right-hand zigzag cones.
- Through the finish gates to end the course.

Setup

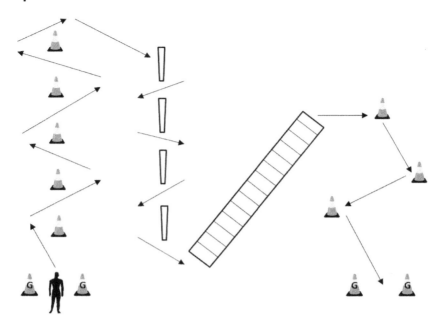

Footlympics: Coloured Batak

Explanation

The final Footlympics event will test a goalkeeper's footwork whilst moving into different positions around the goal.

Aim To accumulate as many points as possible in one minute.

There are two variations to this event using the same setup.

- The coach will call out what coloured cone the goalkeeper will go to.
- The goalkeeper can decide what colour to go to, but they must call the colour before they advance to it.

The goalkeeper will start in between their goal and in front of the starting cone. The coach or the player will call a coloured cone then the goalkeeper will advance to the left firstly, touch this cone, then recover dropping off to the appropriate side. They will then touch the starting cone and do the same to the front set of cones. Once this is done the right side will be worked and the same procedure repeated over and over until the time has elapsed.

The points scoring system goes as follows:

Red = 1 point, Green = 2 points, Yellow = 3 points, Blue = 4 points.

The further away the cone from the starting cone then the higher the points value, apart from the forward facing cones which are all the same value because they are equally spaced from the starting cone.

This event will test a goalkeeper's decision making when it's up to them what colour to go for as well as, of course, their physical speed out of their immediate goal area. When the coach makes the decision for any keeper, then it might be deemed unfair if some participants always get the chance to go to the higher value cones - but this will be up to the coach.

The ball is located where it is so that goalkeepers are encouraged to focus on it, making this event as game realistic as possible - and to practice not turning their back on the ball.

Setup

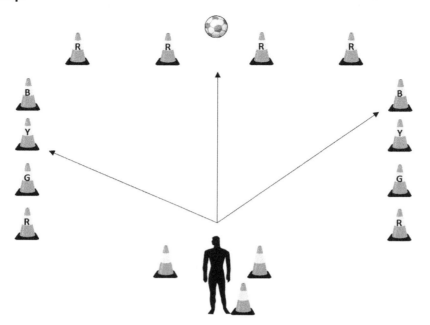

Back Pass

Explanation

The aim here is for the goalkeeper to play the ball through the highlighted areas when receiving a back pass. When the defending team wins the ball, they must attempt to play the ball straight back to the goalkeeper, either directly or by passing to create the opportunity.

If the ball leaves the field of play, a kick in shall be performed. Goal kicks and corners are included and the goalkeeper has the opportunity to hit target areas with a goal kick. After a goal or distribution by the goalkeeper, the coach can decide who and where the play will be restarted to vary the situations faced. If the goalkeeper claims the ball with their hands, they can either throw or drop kick through the target areas.

The attacking team will score a point for a goal and the goalkeeper a point for the target areas. Extra points can be awarded for the further away target areas if desired. Also, a goal against a keeper could result in a point deduction for the goalkeeper.

The circular area is a small sided game, using the other goalkeepers (or outfield players if available).This is usually 2v2 or 3v3 so the working keeper will get plenty of exposure to back passes.

The target areas are located where they are to encourage the goalkeeper to look wide. The areas could be moved depending on your team's tactics or other specifications. Remember – when leaving the width of your goal posts make sure there is eye contact with the player who is playing a back pass to you.

Areas Worked

- Back passes
- Support positions
- Distribution in general
- Tactical understanding
- Verbal/visual communication

Potential Coaching Points

- Are the goalkeeper's support positions appropriate in relation to the ball
- Is their communication effective and informative
- Does the goalkeeper pick the most appropriate options of distribution – in terms of tactical decisions and technique (accuracy, weight of pass)

Game Starting Positions

- Coach plays the ball anywhere into the area – from varying angles
- Let the defending team start with the ball

Example Setup

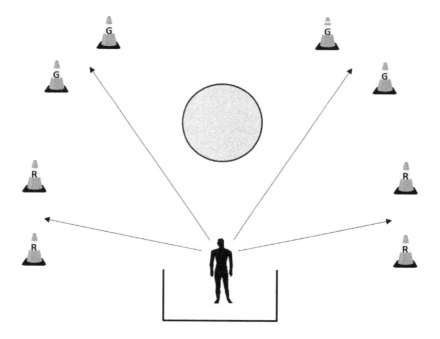

No Bounce

Explanation

The aim of the game is to avoid the ball bouncing in your zone. The team in control of the ball will aim for the opponent's zone (marked out by cones) using an agreed method of distribution. This could be throwing, drop kicks, stationary goal kicks or moving back passes.

If the ball does bounce inside a team's area, the opponents will receive a point and vice-versa. If a ball fails to reach the zone or goes out of play - the ball will go to the other team.

When a goalkeeper gains control, they must distribute the ball within six seconds if it's in their hands. They can gain control by catching the ball directly or controlling it with their body (to replicate a back pass). Try to use one at any time, not both. Keep the game realistic by encouraging the goalkeepers to play quickly.

The example grid can be changed according to the session topic, or a diagonal game can be created to work on distribution into wide areas.

Areas Worked

- All kinds of distribution
- Basic handling
- Teamwork
- Communication

Potential Coaching Points

- Judgement of the ball
- Can the goalkeeper biomechanically perform certain distribution methods
- Look out for technical issues with throwing

Game Starting Positions

- One team starts with the ball
- The coach plays the ball to one of the teams from varying positions
- The coach plays the ball in between the teams' grids – a contest of speed to get the ball is now on

Typical Setup

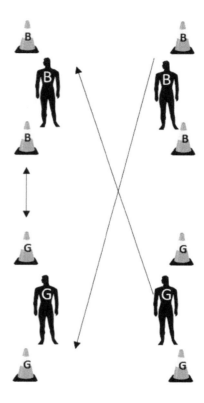

Goalkeeper Bowls

Explanation

The rules are the same as normal bowls with each goalkeeper trying to get their ball nearest the target. It can be played individually (three balls each) or in teams (five balls per team) with the winner the goalkeeper or team getting the ball nearest the target.

The methods of distribution can vary but from experience, the best methods are the underarm roll or the simple pass.

The target can be moved at an angle or distance so a variety of situations can be practised such as hitting the ball to wide areas.

Areas Worked

- Accuracy/weight of distribution

Setup

Distribution Gates

Explanation

The aim of the game is to get the ball through the gates by whatever technique is being practised, for example, goal kicks, throwing, or drop kicks. The gates can be moved closer together to increase difficulty, and they can be moved into different positions or distances from the goalkeeper's start position.

Each goalkeeper will have three turns to accumulate as many points as they can. The one who scores the most points is the winner. The number of turns and balls can vary depending on how many goalkeepers there are in the session.

This is a great game for keepers to learn about distribution and, in my experience, all the goalkeepers who have taken part have felt their distribution had improved and they were able to have a fun, competitive game at the same time.

Areas Worked

- Accuracy/weight of distribution
- Different methods (both feet and arms)

Setup

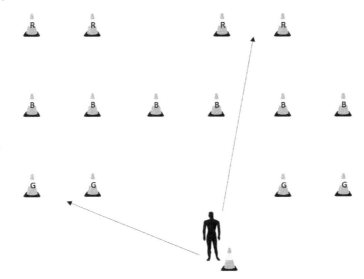

Red = 5 points, Blue = 3 points, Green = 2 points

Accuracy

Explanation

This game uses tennis balls and works on the accuracy of the throw as well as having receiving goalkeepers work on their hand-eye coordination. It's best done indoors, but can also be done on grass and with different types of balls.

All of the distances can vary depending on the age and ability of the goalkeepers. The coach can lay out the game or ask the participants what dimensions they would prefer.

The goalkeepers will throw the ball aiming to bounce it within the red target zone and aiming for an opposition goalkeeper. At first, this is done from a stationary position with the receiver of the ball then aiming to return the ball to a different goalkeeper.

The exercise can be progressed with the opposite goalkeepers moving around as targets and the goalkeeper receiving the ball remaining stationary when throwing.

Another progression can achieved be placing goals or targets for the goalkeepers to hit on the floor (see below).

Areas Worked

- Throwing accuracy
- Hand-eye coordination
- Reactions

Setups

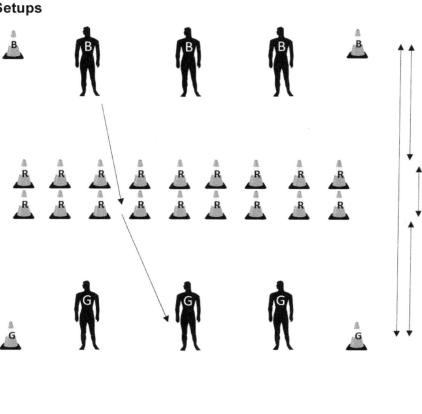

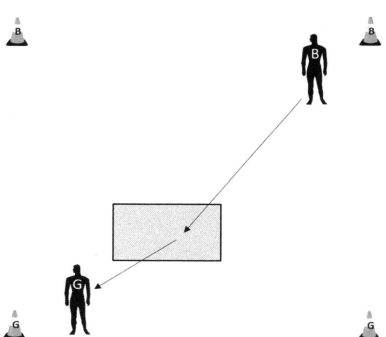

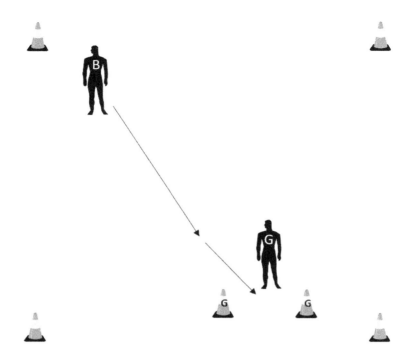

This is a good game to challenge participants and easy to adapt the dimensions and demands according to the group's training needs. Points can be awarded for getting the ball to bounce in the target zone or for scores in a placed goal.

1v1 Situations

Gate Keeper

Explanation

The aim of this game is to get the goalkeeper diving at the feet of the attacker and stopping them getting past. If the attacker gets past the goalkeeper, they dribble through the gate then around the side of the grid and return to the back of the line.

This game focuses on 1v1 situations and how a goalkeeper can stop the attacker getting past them and scoring. The attacker will work on their touch and decision making in this game and finish things off when outside the grid by doing a small exercise before returning to the back of the line. For larger groups, the grid can be made bigger and more than one goalkeeper and attacker can be worked at the same time.

Areas Worked

- Courage (diving at feet)
- Timing of when to commit
- Positioning from starting ball – front foot

Potential Coaching Points

- Is the goalkeeper in an appropriate starting position in relation to the ball being dribbled in
- Does the goalkeeper move/commit when the ball is under control from the attacker
- Delaying and forcing wide
- Working in unison where there are two goalkeepers trying to save the ball

Game Starting Positions

- From the shown gate on the diagram
- Coach plays the ball into the attacker – the goalkeeper(s) will respond off their first touch

Typical Setup

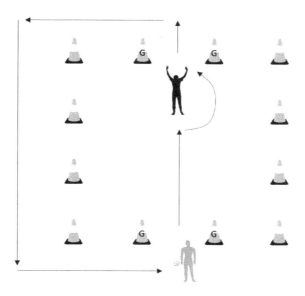

Alternative Setup

The attacker now has a choice, and the goalkeeper will have to adjust accordingly; for example, there are two goals for the attacker to head for.

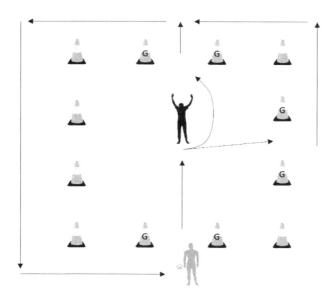

Keeper in the Middle

Explanation

Depending on the number of participants the grid can change size and more than one goalkeeper can be working at a time. The goalkeepers can start by intercepting with their feet but then move on to trying to gain the ball using their hands. This creates a 1v1 situation, and this game would be a good starting point to introduce 1v1 techniques and the skills needed.

A maximum number of touches can be placed on the 'outside goalkeepers' to improve their first touch and composure on the ball.

Areas Worked

- Not committing early
- Timing of interception
- Speed
- Agility

Typical Setup

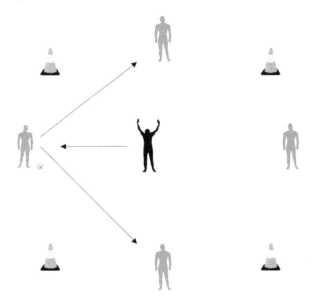

Crocodiles

Explanation

Using two goals in a grid, one team of goalkeepers will be outfield players and one team will play as goalkeepers (with the outfield team overloaded). If a goal is scored, the play will switch and the opposite goal will be attacked.

The aim will be for the outfield players to score and for the normal goalkeepers to intercept or save the ball – an interception or a save will count as a goal if they do.

The idea behind "Crocodiles" is that the goalkeepers are protecting something, in this case a goal - the outfield goalkeepers can't allow the Crocodiles to get the ball as they can't get it back off them!

The outfield goalkeepers use their feet to start with - using passing and dribbling. When the drill progresses, the goalkeepers playing outfield can use their hands to throw and drop kick if required.

Different conditions can be put on the game such as 'two touches maximum' and players will rotate roles once five goals have been achieved by a team.

Areas Worked

- Footwork
- Communication
- Positional play
- Organisation
- Tactics

Potential Coaching Points

- Does the goalkeeper(s) make effective saves
- Does the goalkeeper(s) find a way to prevent the attackers coming too close to the goal
- Does the goalkeeper(s) know when to set
- Diving angles and hand shapes

Game Starting Positions

- Coach plays the ball anywhere into the grid
- Coach plays to the attackers who go for goal
- The goalkeepers start with the ball – distributing the ball to the attackers

Typical Setup

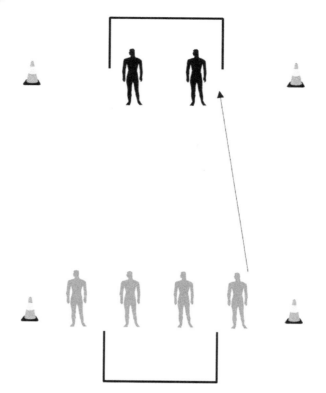

Parallel Goals

Explanation

There are two separate games which the coach will play balls into at random. Either side could be chosen so the goalkeepers must be paying attention and focusing on the ball. When the ball is entered into one side, then the attacking player can go for goal or choose to switch the ball to the other side and play from there.

The roles will be rotated once a goalkeeper has conceded five goals. Or you could swap things to winner-stays-on where conceding two or three goals results in a change.

Areas Worked

- Concentration
- Reaction time

Potential Coaching Points

- Front foot starting position
- Does the goalkeeper re-adjust to the ball played through
- Forcing the attacker out of the playing area

Game Starting Positions

- Coach plays the ball either side of the area

Typical Setup

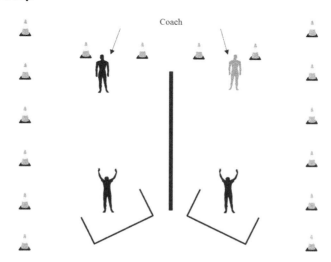

Reaction 1 v 1

Explanation

The ball will start with the server, and they will play a pass into the attacker who will take a shot at either goal they wish. The shot must be first time.

The goalkeeper will try to keep the ball out of the goal using quick reactions. The goalkeeper with the least number of goals scored against them in the allotted time will be the winner.

This can be done as a winner-stays-on game, or the positions can be rotated.

Areas Worked

- Concentration
- Reaction saves
- Fast and strong hands

Typical Setup

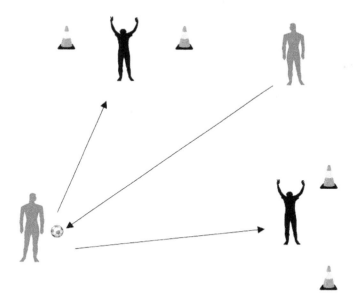

Goals Galore

Explanation

Inside the designated grid (can be smaller when working on 1v1s and reaction saves) there will be a series of mini goals that the goalkeepers will have to defend.

The game can be played with one ball per group and the outfield players passing, or one ball per outfield player.

Each goalkeeper will have his or her own goal and will score a point by making a save and lose a point for a goal conceded. The other non-working goalkeepers will act as outfield players, and their objective is to score. They can do this by dribbling through their goal or passing to a team member (if the game is with one ball).

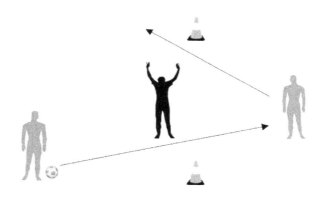

If the goalkeeper gains control of the ball, they will distribute the ball to another player. That player cannot directly score back into that goalkeeper's goal.

If a goal is scored or the ball goes outside the grid - the coach will play another ball into the grid, either to a player or space.

When the designated time is up, the goalkeeper with the most points will be the winner. If the whole group is made up of goalkeepers, then people will swap positions.

Areas Worked

- Concentration
- Reacting to changing situations

Potential Coaching Points

- Staying big to block the goal
- Scanning the field for potential attacks
- Is the goalkeeper ready for attack on their goal
- Can the goalkeeper take the ball when it's out of the attackers' feet

Game Starting Positions

- One attacker starts with the ball
- The coach plays the ball into the area from varying angles and distances
- A goalkeeper starts with the ball and distributes to any attacking player

Example Setup

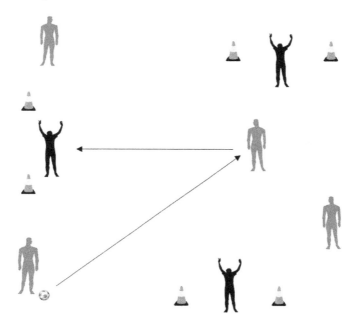

Crossing

Cross Goal

Explanation

There will be a number of servers placed at a variety of different positions around the designated working area - serving crosses. Balls can be thrown or kicked towards the goalkeeper depending on the ability of the group. For the group to get a feel for the exercise - throwing the ball, to start with, might be a good idea.

When a colour is called by the coach the working goalkeeper must touch that coloured cone then move into a position in relation to the ball to be able to claim the cross and stop the ball going into the goal.

The serve order can be determined by working along the line or by issuing numbers; when a colour is called so is a number and the goalkeeper will need to react to the position of that number in relation to the goal area.

To make the exercise more game-based the servers will gain a point for a goal and the goalkeepers for a save or an effective dealing with the cross.

This exercise doesn't have to be game-based if the technique of dealing with crosses hasn't been done by the group before.

Defenders and attackers can be introduced to make the exercise opposed. The example setup looks more at straight crosses – but the position of the crossers can be any width or depth.

Potential Coaching Points

- Re-adjusting position
- The timing of the jumping movement
- Look for all the standard crossing coaching points – e.g. deal with the ball at highest, safest point, etc.

Game Starting Positions

- Each crossing player has a ball
- The crossing players pass a ball between themselves
- The coach gives the goalkeeper a cross, who then distributes the ball to any of the crossing players who control the ball and look to cross.

Example Setup

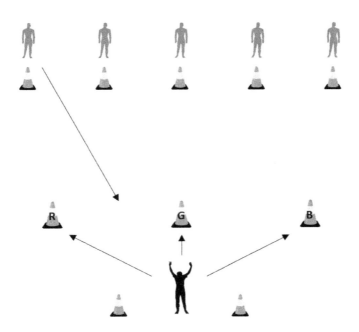

Don't Cross Me!

Explanation

Similar to the original "Cross Goal", the concept here is the same such that the servers will look to produce a delivery that will test the goalkeeper's ability to deal with crossed balls.

The servers will aim to score in the opposite goal, at the far post, making the goalkeeper come and deal with the ball at the far post. The height of the side goals should be the same as the main goal.

The goalkeeper's positioning in relation to the ball and the goal will be important here. Once again attackers and defenders can be added to make the exercise more game realistic.

Typical Setup

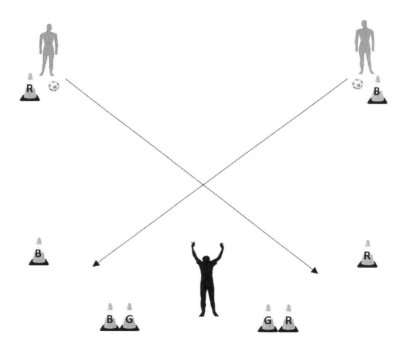

Summary

As discussed before – games-based goalkeeper training is an alternative to the traditional goalkeeping curriculum. The approach also looks to bridge the gap between isolated technical training, and the whole team training environments. This is a potentially neglected area where goalkeepers are proficient in technical practices but then struggle when faced with the reactive and ever changing game environment. The games shown alleviate this transition and are used when the goalkeeping coach takes their sessions.

The games take the goalkeeper out of their comfort zone, and the concept accepts errors and mistakes will be made. From the coach's perspective, these exercises should increase a goalkeeper's ability to figure out appropriate techniques and movements for themselves.

With the diagnostics being done by the goalkeepers and coaches – through questioning and guided discovery – a motivated and relevant learning environment is created. The goalkeepers will be able to self-regulate their own performance making their own judgements and observations to see what works best for them. The coach, by giving different performance cues (coaching points, buzz words, triggers, encouragement or praise for hard work) can help stimulate the goalkeeper and ignite their learning. It is different from the direct model or command style.

If you're planning a session with perhaps two or three games then make sure there are rest periods in between as the intensity of the games can be high – a tip to break the games up would be to break away and do something completely different. I've separated games by small possession exercises or some isolated technical work – such as volleys or shots that work a particular handling technique. Or even watching a video to give the goalkeepers a physical break – but still keep them engaged by doing something fun but at the same time bringing in variation.

A key bit of advice would be to change your coaching position when carrying out the games. This way you will get a great view from different angles – not fixed into one place. This will add variety to the feedback and questioning.

Now you've seen examples of the games go out and use them as a starter! Put your own twists and spin on each game and tailor them to the group you're working with. Your goalkeepers should love them. Every coaching environment I've been involved with has benefited in some way from each of the games. They are a great way to bring a new group together, teach new skills to existing goalkeepers or give an experienced group a taste of something different from the norm.

Bonus Section

Paul Webb heads up the eponymous *Paul Webb Academy* and has been one of the UK's leading strength and conditioning coaches for over 20 years. Paul was originally a goalkeeper and began working with athletes of all levels and abilities when he retired. He is the author of two football-related strength training books.

In this bonus section, Paul discusses a ready-to-run strength training routine for goalkeepers across the age and capability spectrum. It is deliberately designed to be simple and easy to apply, and needs only the minimum of equipment.

Importantly, it targets what *goalkeepers* (and not our outfield compatriots) actually need to develop.

Over to Paul...

Paul Webb

When I was a goalkeeper, it's fair to say that specific training protocols for the most athletic position on the football field – the goalie – were less than ideal.

Running around the pitch, some shuttle runs, handling practice, and shot stopping were our standard 'go to' goalkeeping training!

Fortunately, however, times have changed although some coaches today are still performing endless training sessions that aren't really helping goalkeepers to develop into world class athletes.

Developing the necessary attributes to maximise goalkeeping performance takes time. There are no quick fixes.

The goalkeeper has to commit to practice and self-improvement over a number of years, increasing his or her skill levels in technical areas as well as strength and conditioning.

The following example is just a small part of that overall development journey. The goalkeeper works in short bursts, in multiple directions, and the session has been designed to develop keepers using a bare minimum of equipment.

We are going to perform these individual exercises in a circuit fashion (i.e. one after the other with minimal rest in-between) performing as many repetitions as possible in the allowed time frame with excellent technique.

Perform each exercise for between 30-45 seconds (depending on how fit the athlete is) with a 20-30 second rest between each exercise.

After completing the whole circuit, rest for 60-90 seconds before repeating for a total of 3-4 sets.

The entire workout will look like this:

- Reverse Lunges (alternate between legs) 30 seconds on/20 seconds rest
- Press Ups 30 seconds on/20 seconds rest
- High Knee Run 30 seconds on/20 seconds rest
- Mountain Climbers 30 seconds on/20 seconds rest
- KB Swing 30 seconds on/90 seconds rest before the next set

When working with younger players, ensure that the kettlebells are appropriate to their strength. In turn, do your best to make the circuits fun and fulfilling – youngsters (in particular) will dread strength training if it is a drudge. Make use of light-hearted competition, music, prizes, laughter, and help your athletes really see how much they are improving.

Reverse Lunge

The reverse lunge is good here, as generally it's the version that causes the fewest technical issues! Stand tall and reach back with one foot. As you plant the rear foot, make sure the front foot is completely flat on the ground. *DON'T* hyperextend the lower back (lean back too far) and drive off the front foot to return to the start position. Repeat on the other side...

Press Ups

Yep, the good old fashioned push/press up. Set up with feet together and hands directly under shoulders. *DON'T* allow your elbows to flare out – you want to keep them alongside your body. Tighten everything and slowly lower all the way to the floor. Pause slightly and then drive upwards to the start position...

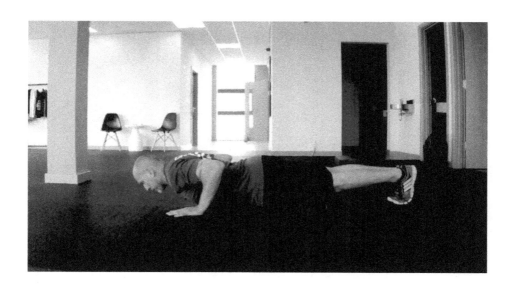

High Knee Run

Effectively a sprint without moving anywhere, drive from the shoulders and get knees as high as possible whilst moving extremely quickly...

Mountain Climbers

Again, start in a push up position and drive one knee at a time towards your chest. Be dynamic with this movement.

Kettlebell Swings

Stand behind a heavy (albeit age appropriate) kettlebell and hinge forward from the hips as you take a grip on the 'bell. Pull the kettlebell back towards your lap and then drive the hips forward explosively whilst keeping a tight grip on the kettlebell handle. Allow the 'bell to swing back and then repeat for desired repetitions...

Summary

So, there you have it. A simple circuit that will actively develop the core muscles and strength that a goalkeeper needs. All the best!

Other Coaching Books

Ray Power's *Deliberate Soccer Practice* Series

- Deliberate Soccer Practice: 50 Defending Football Exercises to Improve Decision-Making
- Deliberate Soccer Practice: 50 Passing & Possession Football Exercises to Improve Decision-Making
- Deliberate Soccer Practice: 50 Attacking Exercises to Improve Decision-Making

Gary Curneen's *Modern Soccer Coach* Series

- The Modern Soccer Coach: Pre-Season Training
- The Modern Soccer Coach 2014: A Four Dimensional Approach
- The Modern Soccer Coach: Position-Specific Training

Dan Abrahams' Soccer Psychology Books

- Soccer Tough: Simple Football Psychology Techniques to Improve Your Game
- Soccer Tough 2: Advanced Psychology Techniques for Footballers
- Soccer Brain: The 4C Coaching Model for Developing World Class Player Mindsets and a Winning Football Team

In fact, we publish lots more coaching books:

- Play Like Pep Guardiola's Barcelona: A Soccer Coach's Guide | Agustín Peraita
- Winning Your Players through Trust, Loyalty, and Respect | DeAngelo Wiser
- Youth Soccer Development: Progressing the Person to Improve the Player | Noel Dempsey
- Let's Talk Soccer: Using Game-Calls to Develop Communication in Football | Gérard Jones
- What is Tactical Periodization? | Xavier Tamarit
- Coaching Psychological Skills in Youth Football: Developing The 5Cs | Chris Harwood and Richard Anderson
- Developing the Modern Footballer through Futsal | Michael Skubala & Seth Burkett
- Soccer Tactics 2014: What the World Cup Taught Us | Ray Power
- Universality - The Blueprint for Soccer's New Era: How Germany and Pep Guardiola Are Showing Us the Future Football Game | Matthew Whitehouse
- Making the Ball Roll: A Complete Guide to Youth Football for the Aspiring Soccer Coach | Ray Power

* * *

Learn More about our Books at: www.BennionKearny.com/Soccer

* * *

CPSIA information can be obtained
at www.ICGtesting.com
Printed in the USA
BVHW01s1711160718
521770BV00001B/1/P

9 781910 773444